Bullshit Bingo

www.southbankpublishing.com

Bullshit Bingo

Graham Edmonds

southbank
publishing

This edition published in 2005 by Southbank Publishing
P.O.Box 394, Harpenden, Herts, AL5 1XJ
www.southbankpublishing.com

A CIP catalogue record for this book is available from the British Library

ISBN 1 904915 14 0

2 4 6 8 10 9 7 5 3 1

Typeset by Avocet Typeset, Chilton, Aylesbury, Bucks
Printed and bound in Great Britain by Cox & Wyman, Reading

Introduction

Welcome to Bullshit Bingo! It's the book that lifts the lid on all the bullshit you hear and see around you, especially in the workplace.

We at Southbank have had our bullshit detectors scouring offices from around the world for the best bullshit words and phrases; we've even looked at the ways bullshit is applied in actions and even with music.

The English language evolves constantly and office culture, with its atmosphere of competitiveness and scope for advancement by bullshit, is a prime breeding ground for new words, phrases, metaphors and euphemisms.

The type of bullshit we're covering in this book is corporate and largely to do with fakery and the attempt to put one over on a competitor to gain favour or to impress.

To the consummate company bullshitter, it's a way of life; he or she is out to impress all the time, to look clever and to use this language to make others appear stupid; this is about their audience and not about accuracy and fair play, or even good business.

It's often amazing to see what bullshitters get away with; their use of language combined with sheer cheek is often fascinating to observers, unless they are on the receiving end of course.

Bullshit language can play a positive role; it can take the aggression out of situations and provide the surreal comedy from which this book has grown.

This book is divided into sections that reflect company departments and activities such as conferences and recruitment. Each comes with a glossary of terms and explanations of how the office bullshitter uses them, plus a Bullshit Bingo card for you to take to the meetings. We've also included some blank cards for you to put together your own or photocopy.

We've also included some fun cards on clichés: sports, *Match of the Day* and *Politics* featuring Jeremy Paxman's interviews.

We love bullshit so much that we'd like yours; if you hear of any new words, clichés, mixed metaphors, euphemisms or phrases that we haven't included in the book, please do let us know what they are and we'll include them in the next edition. E-mail them to bullshit-bingo@southbank.co.uk

Everyone who has ever worked in an office has used bullshit at some time during their working day and we all know those people who live by bullshit. This book is dedicated to them and long may they continue to entertain us, just as long as they don't undermine us.

So eyes down...

BULLSHIT BINGO – The Classics

ON MESSAGE	DUCKS IN A ROW	ENGAGE	DISCONNECT	LAND	JOINED UP THINKING	MAKE IT WORK	BACK TO BASICS	LEVEL PLAYING FIELD	CHERRY PICK
ENERGY	LOW HANGING FRUIT	PARK IT	FOCUS	TEMPLATE	BIG PICTURE	GO FOR IT	LAND MINES	WIN HEARTS AND MINDS	TICK THE BOXES
OFFLINE	GAME PLAN	WIN-WIN	LEARNINGS	FAST TRACK	STRATEGIC	LEARNING CURVE	MANAGE CHANGE	TOUCH BASE	ROBUST
BENCH MARK	BALL PARK	PROACTIVE, NOT REACTIVE	CONNECT	BRAIN STORM	FLIGHT PATH	THE BOTTOM LINE	COOKING WITH GAS	CUSTOMER DRIVEN	PROCESS
GO THE EXTRA MILE	AT THE END OF THE DAY	FEEDBACK	SCOPE	ROCKET SCIENCE	BARRIER	THINK OUTSIDE THE BOX	CLIENT FOCUSED	CUSTOMER FOCUSED	MOVE THE GOAL POSTS
EMPOWER	FRAME WORK	RESULTS DRIVEN	BEST PRACTICE	SYNERGY	QUALITY	SKILL SET	MINDSET	ACTION	BASKET CASE

How to play: simply tick off six words in one meeting and shout out BINGO!

Contents

1. Bullshitters' and fakes' recognised behaviours

"Dressing up is inevitably a substitute for good ideas. It is no coincidence that technically inept business types are known as 'suits'."

Paul Graham

Bullshitters' and fakes' recognised behaviours
Some of the best bullshitters and fakes appear to take on the persona of the company they work for, seamlessly moving from job to job and often getting large pay offs as they are found out, often making a lot of money in the process. Companies are often too embarrassed to admit their mistakes in employing them.

Bullshitting is an art; the right behaviour is vital to success and here are some of the typical tricks of the trade. It's all about getting noticed; watching the way a skilled bullshitter aligns themself to make the most of their position is pretty impressive, even though you may not approve.

Acting important
A real skill, it involves wearing culturally correct clothes, knowing what to say in meetings without actually committing to anything, using the right body language to suggest power and with an attitude that goes with looking completely confident. It involves walking with a purpose, talking slightly loudly and acting in a seemingly very earnest way.

Asking a question while knowing the answer to increase credibility and profile
Sometimes, when this is very cleverly done, the question will be one that enables the boss to shine, allowing the questioner to bask in the reflected glory and to be thought of by the boss in a more positive light.

Being seen around the office
An important prerequisite for anyone who wants to get on, being seen is a must for any attention seeker and go-getter: turning up early when they know it will be noticed or working late when they know the boss is there. Even when not in the office, the best fakes will leave a familiar jacket or bag strategically placed so that it gives the impression they're around somewhere.

Bumping into the boss
It's important to know the boss's schedule, 'bumping' into them in the corridor, lift, loo, or by the coffee machine is a good way to get attention…

Business dress
The best company bullshitters are not necessarily the smartest in the office; they are the ones that dress most like the boss. Alignment by fashion.

'Can do' attitude
The successful manager always projects a 'can do' attitude; it's an essential part of being successful in a large corporation, a little like 'acting important' but with the sleeves rolled up. These people attack every job they are given with verve in the hope that they'll be seen as top management material.

Claiming credit for the work of others
A classic tactic and one regularly practised by unscrupulous bosses everywhere. Claiming credit for the work of others requires skill in

lying outrageously, bare faced cheek, plausibility and the ability to keep a straight face as others react when they realise what is going on.

Clapping
A good way to get attention is to clap with hollowed hands; it's louder and sounds more appreciative.

Copying in select important people on memos and e-mails
This is really an out of date way of attention grabbing as it's such an obvious one, but it still goes on, though possibly now only the province of the desperate.

Creating a problem to solve the problem
One of the most difficult bullshit activities to spot, but one of the most common, typically the corporate bullshitter will call a meeting with their boss and team to discuss a problem that most of them didn't know existed. The team will be dispatched to 'fix the problem' and after a suitable time has elapsed and with no success by the team, the bullshitter will leap into action to solve the problem, neatly appearing to the boss as a saviour and promotion candidate.

Dissing ex-colleagues
When someone leaves the company, the office fake will arrange it so that their own mistakes can be attributed to the one who left. Those returning to a company they have previously left should be aware.

Empire building
A term used to describe people who expand their teams and take on bigger areas of responsibility in an attempt to appear indispensable. It's also a good ploy for getting a pay rise as the bigger the team, the more you should earn. **Featherbedding** is an old term from the days when unions had such power they could pressure companies to employ more people than they actually needed to perform a specific task. The bullshitter uses the same technique to make it look like their

teams are bigger than they really are; therefore the manager is more important and deserves their big pay packet.

Employ someone to take the heat then sack them for failure or take credit for their success

Typically the company bullshitter will have been given an important task; they will then employ someone to do the work, neatly ensuring that if it goes wrong, there's someone sackable in place to take the blame and, if it's a success, the fake can still present the work as their own.

Finding out the boss's interests

Is the boss a fan of Prog Rock or Hip Hop? Do they read Dickens or Dan Brown? The bullshitter will find out and spookily become fans of the same.

Gadgetry

Providing the boss is technically aware, being seen with the latest handheld PC will look good, while the right mobile phone is essential; it must look good and have a ring tone that isn't tacky but shows some sophistication, so more Coldplay than Cheeky Girls.

Holding something

Files, clipboards and laptops are all essential office accessories; even holding a sheaf of paper makes you look more important, especially if you're reading it intently as you walk. Real aficionados will have files marked 'for MD's eyes only'.

Ignoring what's right

A sure sign of a bullshitter and someone who is only looking after number one is when a situation arises where there is one obvious course of action. The fake will ignore it and do what is right for them and their career. It's about looking right, not being right.

Jargon use
Every company has its own jargon and culture, usually reflective of their management; the skilled corporate bullshitter will take on the language and terminology, firstly to fit in, then to impress.

Laughing loudly at an unfunny joke made by a director or senior manager
A sad activity, it just encourages them to make more bad jokes.

Praising the boss
One of the oldest in the book, but it works, the skilled bullshitter will not be too over the top as it can lead to disaster.

Putting the bullshitter's name in the footnotes of presentations and spreadsheets
A common trick; even if the culprits didn't do the work, it looks like they did.

Sex
Sexy people are the best bullshitters; all their victims think about is how gorgeous they are and all the time they're undermining them, with their short skirts, tight bums and winning smiles…and that's just the men.

Summarising the boss's ideas and feeding it back to them
The skilled bullshitter will listen to what their boss has to say, pull out the salient opinions and replay it all back to them using similar words. This gives the impression that they are on the same side as the boss and understand fully what he or she wants. Faking empathy is a great skill; it can appear insincere but when it works it's very effective.

Swearing to give credibility
Using four letter words to give a bit of cred was very much a male pastime but now women engage in this too in an attempt to be 'one

of the boys' or to prove how tough they can be. Whoever it is, the user is marked as a bullshitter.

Taking the lead during presentations

'You're only as good as your last presentation' is a motto often followed by the most successful fakes. Have you ever noticed how the best presenters always get on?

Talking loudly

One for open plan offices, the technique is to wait for the boss to be around, then be heard talking on the phone using words and phrases like 'the numbers', 'deal', 'contract' or 'customer'. These should be bandied about along with sideways glances to see that the boss is listening.

Walking purposefully

The walk is very important; it is essential to look like an important mission is involved, one that is vital to the future of the company. Ideally you must carry a clipboard or piece of paper, though the real aficionados will be walking round with envelopes marked 'For Chairman's eyes only' or 'Confidential'.

2. Leaders and managers

"Leadership is the art of getting someone else to do something
you want done because he wants to do it."

Dwight D Eisenhower

Leaders and managers
Leaders and managers speak to their teams in certain ways but there
are many different types and styles. Most work in their own ways, but
here we look at the characteristics of the leader and how they are most
likely to bullshit you, the team member or junior executive.

Leadership
According to business guru Peter Drucker, the four key competences
of a leader are as follows:

Listening
Communicating
Not to use alibis
The realisation that the leader is less important than the task in hand.

We have a fifth...

Bullshitting, whether Drucker likes it or not, is what's needed to get
on in the real world.

Remember these when next dealing with your boss.

The business guru and the media have created several types of leader and also recognisable traits; here are our interpretations plus a few added that we've learned about along the way….

Articulate inadequate
Looks great, sounds great and knows nothing.
Motto – looking good.

Chameleon
Out for themselves and no one else, a bullshitter par excellence will change views to whatever they feel is the prevailing one or the one that gives them best advantage.
Motto – what's your view?

Churchillian
Great in a battle, defensive, always right and with very high morals.
Motto – V is for victory (the Churchill family motto is Fiel Pero Desdichado – Faithful but unfortunate).

Conflict avoider
Hates any sort of argument, doesn't really like people and manages the team by e-mail to avoid contact.
Motto – anything you like really.

Deal junkie
Just likes doing deals, no leadership skills whatsoever, will turn everything into a negotiation.
Motto – come on, let's discuss this, we're in a partnership here…

Easy going, nice
Not bothered about deadlines, will use terms like **end of play** instead of 'I want it on my desk by 4p.m.', a manager to be taken advantage of. Never successful, too well liked and not ruthless enough.
Motto – sure, whatever…

Fad surfer

A manager that adopts each trend in management as it appears, a bit of a bullshitter then...

Motto – whatever sounds right at the time.

Family, Mum or Dad

Sees their team as their children, very protective, slightly embarrassing and a little mad.

Motto – we're in this together (and means it).

Fighter

Argumentative, protective and people will say about them that 'you'd want him/her by your side in a fight'. Leads from the front.

Motto – COME ON!

Flatterer

Compliments, unctuousness and general ability to arse lick.

Motto – you look just fantastic...

Geezer

A British phenomenon, they want to give the impression that they're streetwise, hard and a bit of a lad...but everyone knows that they're really from Guildford.

Motto – no motto but liberal use of words like *duckin' and divin', pukka, innit* will mark them out.

Goal-oriented

There's a target for everything...

Motto – right, what's next?

Hard

They're tough and overly competitive.

Motto – don't take prisoners.

Impatient
Always stressed, inefficient, always missing deadlines.
Motto – I need it yesterday.

Indecisive
Can't make up their mind, obsessive tinkering with plans and ideas.
Motto – yes and no, maybe…

Inspirational
True leader and when you're with them you feel great, usually no substance beyond the obvious, tell you only good things.
Motto – we can do it, together we're a great team…

Lazy
Couldn't care less what happens, hoping for the sack and a good pay off.
Motto – I think you're mistaking me for someone who gives a shit.

Look at me
Always the first up, takes credit for the work of the team, ruthless.
Motto – me, me, me.

Machiavellian
A political, cunning, deceitful little weasel.
Motto – one goal, my goal.

Mentor
Wise and trusted, great for advice.
Motto – I'll look after you.

Mushroom
Keeps the team in the dark and feeds them shit.
Motto – information is power.

Numbers
Can't do anything without a spreadsheet to hand.
Motto – I love Excel.

Pervert
Wouldn't want to meet them in a dark alley.
Motto – no motto, just a mirror and a pair of good binoculars.

Power mad, empire builder
Always empire building, always in competition with everyone else.
Motto – the more people in my team, the more power I have...

Process
Manages by the rule book, no imagination, doesn't take risks.
Motto – according to the manual.

Psychopath, sadist
Loves to watch their team suffer, just for fun, nice with it.
Motto – and how are you today?

Puppy dog
Wants to be liked, will agree to and say anything just to be popular,
useless manager as this style leads to lots of arguments within their
team.
Motto – that's a great idea, well done.

Risk averse
Another common type, they won't make commitments in case it
backfires on them, similar to the Indecisive but won't entertain new
ideas at all.
Motto – we'll pass on it this time...

Ruthless
Quiet, shows no mercy and enjoys being a complete shit, not likeable,
no personality.
Motto – no compassion, no mercy.

Savvy
Always aware of what's going on, streetwise and a player.
Motto – understand…

Schizoid
Says one thing, means another and does something else.
Motto – they'll never know…or maybe they will…

Seagull
Flies overhead, makes a lot of noise, lands, shits on the team and flies off when the going gets tough.
Motto – see you later…

Sensitive soul
Cares deeply and manages the team by e-mail in case they say something nasty.
Motto – are you OK? It's not me is it?

Slide-rule
The analytical and intellectual approach to management.
Motto – according to my analysis…

Snooper
This person manages by personal intrusiveness, prying and spying – it's called **snoopervison**.
Motto – really, and what else did they say?

Stepford manager
Looks great, sounds great and agrees with everyone, slightly robotic, perfect tan.
Motto – I concur.

Strategy man
Just sees the wider view, can't do detail.
Motto – OK you can take it from here…

Stress monkey
Always in a panic, everything is a nightmare, transmits stress to their team, a member of staff will eventually hit back.
Motto – Oh my God, it's a nightmare!

Tactician
Thinking is short term only, no ability to think ahead.
Motto – do it now.

Thatcher
A woman who operates like a man in the mould of PM Margaret Thatcher; huge ability, outstanding presentational skills, high work levels and no life outside work, her home is run like her company.
Motto – if you want something said, ask a man; if you want something done, ask a woman.

The 404
From the Internet error message, mistake prone and basically dumb.
Motto – oh shit.

Troubleshooting
So busy solving other people's problems, doesn't do any actual managing of their own team.
Motto – you don't want to do it like that, do it like this...

Wannabe
Completely driven by their ambitions, self interested, sycophantic.
Motto – you're great you are, just great...

Wimp
Completely dominated by their team, unable to cope with leading.
Motto – you do it.

Workaholic
Does everyone's work for them, doesn't trust anyone enough to actually delegate.
Motto – I'll do it.

Yorkshire
I know what I like and I like what I bloody well say…
Motto – I know what I like and I like what I bloody well say…

Inspiring and managing the troops

In these next few sections, you'll find many of the most common terms used by managers to get their teams or individuals to do something…next stop: bullshit city.

Advice, encouragement and attention seeking

As a newcomer trying to make a mark, you often get advice from old sages, mentors, well-meaning colleagues and of course bullshitters who are trying to set you up. Here are some of the classics.

Abandonment
Meaning – leaving, letting go.
Bullshit – in other words, know what to take on and what to leave aside, a key management skill or the sign of a lazy git?

Align, alignment
Meaning – ally oneself, almost agree but not so that you can't backtrack later.
Bullshit – a useful word, especially in confrontational situations. 'Are we aligned on this?' allows people who don't wholly agree with the proposition to save face. A New Labour word…in practice it means decisions are just postponed, hidden and actions taken outside the public arena.

Bang the drum
Meaning – make a fuss, get publicity, get the message over, promote, get things moving and so on.
Bullshit – in the world of the office, this is not about the company, it's about the bullshitter…

Benchmarking
Meaning – comparing to specific or agreed standards, comparing the practices used in other companies in order to improve performance.
Bullshit – a classic bullshit term as it can be used to demonstrate breadth of experience and ability to see the wider view. Used by consultants to extend their contracts. 'We'll have to benchmark extensively so that we can get a holistic view of the market in all its guises. This work should take us, oh a year.' See also *Best practice*.

Bennies
Meaning – a benny is an amphetamine taken as a stimulant; giving the impression that you've taken your bennies is a good thing.
Bullshit – so now you know what a manager means when he asks whether you've taken your bennies this morning. Tell him to fuck off and maybe he'll think you really have.

Best practice
Meaning – the most appropriate way of doing something.
Bullshit – managers that talk about best practice are often deeply insecure, relying on copying the success of others to improve their business. This means that, in reality, they know little about their own business. When this becomes common parlance in a company, then it's time to leave. See also *Benchmarking*.

Bootstrapped
Meaning – to complete something successfully without outside help or by one's own efforts.
Bullshit – a nightmare for the company bullshitter because they can't take credit for it.

Carve out a niche
Meaning – find a place where you will be valued, or a skill you will be known for.
Bullshit – it's good advice to become associated with something good, although too many are given the niche by more experienced managers who like to keep out of trouble. 'Take this project' they will say, 'it will be the making of you.' Not.

Comfort zone
Meaning – an environment or situation in which a person feels secure; they feel comfortable as long as there is no drastic change. New managers are encouraged to get out of their comfort zones and take risks…
Bullshit – many middle managers spend their lives secure in their comfort zone while many others try their best to move them out of it.

Converting plans to action
Meaning – doing what you planned to do.
Bullshit – many companies bang on about what plans they have without ever achieving any of them, eventually though it gets noticed…

Custodian
Meaning – someone who owns or looks after an aspect of the business, see also *Stakeholder*.
Bullshit – basically a self important twat.

Don't rock the boat; don't make waves
Meaning – don't make trouble.
Bullshit – usually said to a difficult member of a team by their manager in an effort to keep the team working together. Probably a good thing if all you want is to get yourself to middle management and stay there.

Easy tiger
Meaning – calm down, don't rush in.
Bullshit – the company bullshitter will be suspicious of enthusiastic, hard-working people; they have the potential to show them up, do a good job and get results. This has to be stopped and 'easy tiger' will be used in a matey way to calm the worker down and restore order to the bullshitter's life. Also listen out for **you can't boil the ocean all at once...**

Excited
Meaning – aroused, enthusiastic, keen, stirred.
Bullshit – know that when a manager tells you they are genuinely 'excited by this opportunity', they usually are just not.

Eyes and ears
Meaning – observant, prying, spy.
Bullshit – you know you're in trouble when your manager says 'I want you to be my eyes and ears on this one.' Someone is being set up.

Fast track
Meaning – to push something or someone through a process faster than usual, the fastest route to a goal.
Bullshit – in reality, everything and everyone is attempting to fast track, which means nothing actually gets done faster.

Final piece of the jigsaw
Meaning – last piece in place, part of a bigger plan.
Bullshit – if you are described as the last piece of the jigsaw, watch out, most companies work on a last in, first out principle.

Food chain
Meaning – a competitive hierarchy derived from the biological system where the weak are preyed upon by the strong. **Survival of the fittest** is also often heard in this context.
Bullshit – getting to the top of the corporate food chain is the goal of most company bullshitters, or at the very least, the top in their little pond.

Free ride
Meaning – easy time, something for nothing.
Bullshit – many managers are looking for a free ride and some old lags are great at looking good while their teams are slaving away on their behalf.

Go the extra mile, sweat harder
Meaning – do more than is expected.
Bullshit – 'if you go the extra mile, you'll be noticed and get on'; in other words, you'll do more work and the manager will get the credit.

Grasp the nettle
Meaning – take the opportunity without fear, even though it may hurt a bit.
Bullshit – it will hurt a lot actually. This is best said in a Welsh accent.

Gravitas
Meaning – substance, weight, standing, dignity and respect.
Bullshit – developing gravitas is very desirable among leaders, although it can look like they're just **acting important**.

Grown up
Meaning – adult, mature.
Bullshit – along with **acting important** and **gravitas**, it's important to appear to take things seriously; being childish or funny is seen as immature and not a good career move no matter how tempting it is. Ha!

Halo effect
Meaning – one great achievement, trait or benefit that gives a favourable view to the whole.
Bullshit – often those good at presentations get on well because of the halo effect, the logic being that if they are good at presentations, it therefore means they're good at everything else too, until reality bites and everyone realises that they were just good at presentations.

Hidden agenda
Meaning – an undisclosed plan, usually with an ulterior motive.
Bullshit – the hidden agenda is integral to the human condition.

Hit the ground running
Meaning – start fast, know what you're doing without training.
Bullshit – managers like people who can do this; it saves time and energy on training and leaves them to do other things, like stitch up their boss for example.

Hungry, lean and mean
Meaning – eager, keen for work.
Bullshit – equals gullible.

I didn't get where I am today by…
A saying made famous in the Reginald Perrin TV series and probably not said out loud much today, but virtually every senior manager today, when confronted by a young pretender, will think it.

Incentives, Fruits of success
Meaning – rewards, bonuses and the promise of promotion.
Bullshit – funny how often it's mentioned – **keep your eye on the prize** they'll say; usually there's some reason for it not to be paid or that promotion not to happen.

Influencer
Meaning – people who have the ability to influence others successfully.
Bullshit – companies love and hate influencers in equal measures, they know they need them but don't trust them.

In the boss's boat/canoe
Meaning – one of the chosen few, a sign of possible promotion.
Bullshit – a good sign, you're in their team and one of the chosen few. Of course if things go wrong and they get the sack, you could go down with them…

It's a jungle out there
Meaning – a visual allegory for a place characterized by intense and ruthless competition or the struggle for survival.
Bullshit – watch your step, in some companies it's true!

Knowledge, Know-how
Meaning – acquiring experience, expertise and skills, the **knowledge base** and the **knowledge worker** are common terms.
Bullshit – knowledge is a powerful thing, protect knowledge and use it wisely. The greater the knowledge acquired, the better the bullshit.

Learnings
Meaning – lessons learnt, knowledge acquired.
Bullshit – usually when something goes awry and the manager in question wants to appear collected, 'I know it's gone wrong, but what are the learnings we can take away from this experience?' Sometimes it's **lessons learned, key learnings** or **learning points**, either way, despite the fact they're swearing their heads off inside, they appear wise and in control.

Levels of honesty
Meaning – don't tell lies but don't always give out the entire truth, being selective about what information is given.
Bullshit – don't be too honest, it doesn't pay, rule one in the bullshitter's manual.

A lick and a promise
Meaning – a superficial attempt.
Bullshit – many company bullshitters are superficial, applying as little work as they can get away with, with the promise that you will do a better job at a later stage, in fact whole careers have been built on this premise.

Lifeblood
Meaning – a vital part (of a business), for example, staff.
Bullshit – an essential term in the use of flattery to any employee or team, listen out for **salt of the earth** too.

Long haul
Meaning – in for a long period of time, committed.
Bullshit – these days few people are in it for the long haul, although many pretend they are, and are able to build good financial packages on that basis.

Manage expectations
Meaning – keep expectations realistic, no surprises.
Bullshit – managing expectations and bullshit go hand in hand.

Managing upwards
Meaning – to control one's manager.
Bullshit – a key skill for any purveyor of bullshit, it's often what bullshitting is all about.

No is not in my vocabulary
Meaning – always positive, always finds a way to solve a problem.
Bullshit – to any manager who says this ask: 'so you *are* an arse licking wanker then?'

No pressure
Meaning – easy going, stress free.
Bullshit – 'no pressure' they will say, either they're setting you up to fail or they don't give a shit.

On a roll
Meaning – sustained success.
Bullshit – usually the time when companies start to convince themselves of their genius and the time to get out.

On the map
Meaning – make a name for yourself.
Bullshit – get known for something, anything, even if it's someone else's work.

Outcome or results driven
Meaning – towards a specific outcome, by implication this is done with high levels of concentration.
Bullshit – to become an insensitive, single minded shit…

Power lunch, working breakfast
Meaning – working over a meal.
Bullshit – it's been a while since Gordon Gecko declared that 'lunch is for wimps' but many managers and workers work through lunchtimes and other meal times too. Feel for them, for they do not appreciate that they will get no thanks.

Prioritise
Meaning – finding precedence for tasks, usually established by order of importance or urgency.
Bullshit – what is order of importance: making money, profit or keeping the boss happy? You decide.

Proactive
Meaning – to anticipate and act with forethought instead of waiting for something to happen.
Bullshit – equals clever dick.

Produce the goods (and you'll be OK)
Meaning – get results.
Bullshit – usually a feature of aggressive managers who work by inference rather than outright threats.

Profile
Meaning – exposure, renown in the business, reputation.
Bullshit – for any company bullshitter, profile is extremely important; concerned managers and mentors will advise young colleagues to do anything to get noticed, usually this doesn't involve working hard or getting results – making a good presentation to the senior managers is usually enough.

Radar
Meaning – in this context, awareness, to get attention.
Bullshit – making the boss aware is to get on his or her radar; anything they don't know about is under the radar, which often is a great place to be.

Retaliation, getting it in first
Meaning – get your own back.
Bullshit – paranoia rules? Get your coat and go. See **Revenge techniques**.

Robust
Meaning – strong, with stamina.
Bullshit – plans must be robust, staff must be robust, successful bullshit must be robust too.

Sink or swim
Meaning – to fail or succeed without any alternatives.
Bullshit – I don't give a shit how you get on, I can find a replacement and I can't be bothered to train you…

Squeaky clean
Meaning – untarnished, almost too clean.
Bullshit – to be cynical about people who have this image is probably about right, but some try to achieve an astonishingly high level of cleanliness nonetheless.

Straight answer
Meaning – the honest truth without gloss.
Bullshit – people avoid giving a straight answer because it gets them into trouble or it hurts someone they like, it's as simple as that. In a recent survey in the US, it was found that 90% of Americans lied regularly.

Strong work ethic
Meaning – compulsion to be a hard worker.
Bullshit – they're gonna love you…sucker.

Tasking
Meaning – doing specific tasks.
Bullshit – managers who **task** their team with **deliverables** and **goals** generally need locking up.

Tenacious
Meaning – holding fast, not giving up easily.
Bullshit – a good quality but most people are thinking 'oh for god's sake, give it a rest…'

Time management
Meaning – the art of best use of time.
Bullshit – generally a case of do as I say and not what I do, most senior managers get a PA to manage their time, go to the shops, pick the kids up from school, baby-sit and so on.

What can you bring to the party (or table)?
Meaning – what relevant skills have you got?
Bullshit – if you haven't got anything to give, then what are you doing here?

Will to win
Meaning – competitive, strong, don't like losing.
Bullshit – managers love their teams to develop a strong competitive

streak as long as it's not aimed at them, while most company bullshitters are highly competitive but are able to disguise their will to win effectively, but don't be fooled, they're out to get you.

Work life balance
Meaning – the harmony between working and home life.
Bullshit – you'll be expected to work long hours and give up holidays and weekends; the trick is to look like you put in the time. Study your boss's working habits; be there at the same times. This only works if your boss is a bit of a skiver; if he's a workaholic, you've had it.

Work smarter
Meaning – to give more thought to your work, use your intelligence more proactively.
Bullshit – will anyone explain what exactly working smarter means in practice? No, thought not.

You can do it if you believe you can
Meaning – an attempt to build confidence in a team member who has a difficult task.
Bullshit – it should be followed by 'because I can't be arsed'.

You scratch my back and I'll scratch yours… Quid pro quo
Meaning – you do me a favour and I'll do you one.
Bullshit – don't do it!

Managing the team
So it's time to talk to the team, the management wants you to get them on their side…get **back on track, into the game, from the side-lines and on to the pitch** and so on…

What clichés and phrases will you use? Here's some, take your pick, but watch out, they have heard them before, even used a few…

Back on the coal face, at the sharp end

Meaning – the 'coal face' is usually applied to the point where customers meet the company, a shop for example. Someone who works at head office is often described as lacking experience at the 'coal face'. The same applies to the sharp end.

Bullshit – managers will use this term as a badge to improve their credibility and as a euphemism for hard graft or a **back to basics** approach.

Cocks on the block

Meaning – if it goes wrong, we're all for the chop…

Bullshit – particularly unappealing to men, usually said with a slight wince and sounds particularly good if said with an upper class English accent…by a woman.

Consensual bollocks

Meaning – you don't have to agree, just do as I say…I haven't time to mess about discussing things. No time for discussion with others.

Bullshit – a term used by strong leaders who can't stand to debate or have an inability to work in a collegiate way. So that's nearly all of them then.

Dance round the handbags

Meaning – prevaricate, put off making a decision, 'stop dancing round your handbags and get on with it…', borrowed from the dance floor habit of piling up the handbags in the centre of the group.

Bullshit – the favourite of impatient managers everywhere.

Disseminate

Meaning – spread.

Bullshit – in the business world, people don't 'tell' or 'give' out information, they disseminate it, it sounds much more important.

Dovetail

Meaning – to join together perfectly.

Bullshit – often an illusion as the joints are nearly always creaky.

Do you read me?
Meaning – do you understand?
Bullshit – a favourite of aggressive senior managers who think that their staff are illiterate, don't listen or just don't understand when they offer a simple instruction, its use usually only highlights their own stupidity.

Ducks in a row
Meaning – present a united front; be well organised and equally informed. It's all about preparation.
Bullshit – a classic, associated with arse covering and generally said in a way that blame is diverted away from the user. Another famous phrase, **singing from the same hymn sheet**, means much the same thing.

Explore the options
Meaning – look at ways of getting out of a particular situation.
Bullshit – the company bullshitter is always exploring the options and looking for opportunities to shaft colleagues.

Feels like we're in the right place
Meaning – more or less right or nearly there.
Bullshit – vague assertions dominate business life, the speaker really hasn't a clue and is waiting for one of the team to come up with the answer.

Get our act together
Meaning – stop making mistakes and get it right.
Bullshit – a sure sign of desperation if this gets used, either that or the manager is a bit of a softie and it's the first stage towards an eventual bollocking.

Heads up
Meaning – a warning.
Bullshit – 'we must give a heads up to the team', meaning something is going wrong and I want them to get me out of the deep shit I'm already in.

Holding our nerve
Meaning – not being panicked into taking unnecessary actions.
Bullshit – difficult to achieve as the natural reaction to any problem is to try to solve it, unless you're a lazy git, then holding your nerve should come naturally.

Jump through hoops
Meaning – to go to great efforts, derived from circus animals doing tricks.
Bullshit – another cliché used to encourage the team to do more, although it's usually said as 'I'm not asking you to jump though hoops'; in other words, that's exactly what's expected.

Keep it simple
Meaning – 'do the basics well and you'll get a result…'
Bullshit – '…because you're too stupid to do anything more complicated.'

Policy of no surprises
Meaning – take everything into account, predicting all that could go wrong.
Bullshit – an absolute joke but some managers actually believe this is achievable.

Ramp it up, ratchet it up, pump up the volume, pull out all the stops
Meaning – to increase, do significantly better, with immediate effect.
Bullshit – a range of phrases and exhortations bordering on pleas, often said as part of last minute panic as a deadline looms…

Riding the razor blade
Meaning – close to failure, with disastrous results if it all goes wrong.
Bullshit – one of those phrases, like **cocks on the block** or **going tits up** that brings a wince when you think about it too much.

Seamless
Meaning – without breaks, efficient.
Bullshit – no breaks, effective communication, a vision of harmony and the impression that all is well – that's bullshit for you.

Segue
Meaning – smooth transition (pronounced seg way).
Bullshit – well it sounds great and in the manager's mind, works in theory, see *Seamless*.

Stoke up the boiler, boiler room
Meaning – the boiler room is the so called 'hub' of any business, where decisions are made and the real work is done. Stoking it up is encouraging the workers to work harder.
Bullshit – the suckers.

Tactics
Meaning – set of manoeuvres engaged in to achieve a goal.
Bullshit – corporate politics, management, doing business, career planning, bullshit, it's all about tactics really.

Think outside the box, Think outside the square
Meaning – think laterally; solve a problem by taking a different approach to the norm.
Bullshit – these sayings come into play when managers run out of ideas and by encouraging their team to think differently, they hope that something positive will happen. Most of the team meanwhile will be thinking 'what box?'

Wake up and smell the coffee…
Meaning – an exhortation to become aware of something big that's happening…
Bullshit – usually used when a manager wants to rouse their team from some form of lethargy, used too often though and the team just takes the piss.

We're going tits out on this one…
Meaning – going all out, without holding anything back.
Bullshit – women in the team just love this, not.

When the going gets tough, the tough get going
Meaning – the strong always rise to the challenge.
Bullshit – one for the Churchillian style managers, to be said when the team is under pressure, usually with a clenched fist punching the invisible foe. Try not to laugh.

Within our gift
Meaning – it's up to us, only we can get it wrong.
Bullshit – no, it's not, it's down to you, at least when it comes to finding someone to blame when it goes wrong.

Word on the streets
Meaning – what's going on, the latest news, gossip.
Bullshit – any good manager will know what's going on; any good bullshitter will be creating the 'word'.

Working in silos
Meaning – teams working independently, without knowledge of what colleagues are doing.
Bullshit – a true sign of a company dominated by bullshit, time to go when teams aren't working together…

Working party, Workshop
Meaning – a team whose efforts are directed at one project.
Bullshit – these are fine, it's when it becomes a **hothouse** or a **skunk works** then you have to start worrying.

You don't have to be mad to work here but it helps…
Meaning – an old office sign not seen much these days, implying that the working environment is wacky and fun.
Bullshit – if you see this sign in an office, you know that it won't be

wacky or fun, just full of sad individuals convincing themselves it's happy. Get your coat and go.

You guys...
Meaning – you people.
Bullshit – said when the speaker wants to appear non-confrontational and inclusive...watch out!

Meetings
Whatever the situation, invariably you have to have a meeting about it and meetings are often where the show-offs appear and there is the smell of bullshit in the air.

It's not unusual for executives to find themselves spending all day moving from meeting to meeting without getting any real work done...watch out for those using terms like **back to back** or **diary whiteout**; they're either very busy or avoiding work.

Companies have tried to cut meeting times to a minimum with initiatives such as no-meeting Fridays and taking chairs out of the meeting rooms, but they haven't faced up to the fact that many workers actually enjoy being in meetings all day, it means that they don't have to take responsibility or do anything that may backfire on them, like actual work for example.

Circling, to circle with
Meaning – to meet and have a discussion.
Bullshit – sounds quite sinister, as in vultures and vampires.

Docking day/meeting
Meaning – a description for a meeting where two parties working on the same project or industry meet to compare notes and generally catch up with what's going on.
Bullshit – it's obviously much more important to 'dock' than just to have any ordinary meeting.

Energy levels
Meaning – from physics, the state of energy.
Bullshit – what leaders want in meetings is high energy levels, they want a buzz, activity and the feeling that something positive is happening even when it isn't.

Face time
Meaning – time together.
Bullshit – one of the stupidest alternative expressions for a meeting, how about smack in the face time? In the US, this is seen as the time people spend just showing their face around the office.

Feedback
Meaning – the return of information and opinion.
Bullshit – anyone who asks for feedback generally doesn't want to hear the truth, so make them feel better, lie.

Handbags
Meaning – literally a purse, but in this context it's a minor argument, the vision to conjure with is two women fighting ineffectively with their handbags.
Bullshit – the real trick is to avoid an escalation from handbags to weapons of mass destruction.

Huddle
Meaning – an informal meeting.
Bullshit – in some companies, they have huddles instead of meetings, bless.

Share and air
Meaning – give your views, listen to those of others.
Bullshit – watch what you share, others may use it against you…remember **levels of honesty, tactics** and above all, the company bullshitter will be listening.

Swerving
Meaning – getting out of the way.
Bullshit – or avoiding meetings.

Talking shop
Meaning – where nothing happens except discussion.
Bullshit – this applies to most meetings in large companies and many small ones too.

Touch base
Meaning – get together, catch up with each other.
Bullshit – one of the most hated terms in business and rightly so, it should be banned.

Verbal diarrhoea
Meaning – talking nonsense.
Bullshit – for those people who talk just to make a noise, to get noticed and who just bang on and on…

Wallpaper the meeting
Meaning – including a dominance of people who are favourable to one position in order to get something pushed through.
Bullshit – feels like the usual state of affairs then.

Window
Meaning – opportunity.
Bullshit – 'I have a window for you at…' is just one of the most bloody annoying phrases.

Yes but what's the action?
Meaning – what are we going to do?
Bullshit – use of the word action aside, it's usually a moment of great joy when an ineffective manager is asked this question with the team looking expectantly for a reply and, with mouth opening and closing like a fish, he or she says 'can we come back to that?'

BULLSHIT BINGO – Manager's styles

ARTICULATE INADEQUATE	DEAL JUNKIE	CHAMELEON	CONFLICT AVOIDER	NUMBERS	CHURCHILLIAN	EASY GOING NICE	FAD SURFER
SAVVY	SEAGULL	SLIDE-RULE	STRESS MONKEY	STRATEGY MAN	TACTICIAN	MUM OR DAD	WORKAHOLIC
FLATTERER	MUSHROOM	INDECISIVE	INSPIRING	HARD	IMPATIENT	PERVERT	GEEZER
POWER MAD	PROCESS	PSYCHOPATH SADIST	LAZY	TROUBLE SHOOTER	GOAL-ORIENTED	THE 404 (ERROR PRONE)	MACHIAVELLIAN
SCHIZO	PUPPY DOG	WANNABE	STEPFORD	RUTHLESS	WIMP	SNOOPER	RISK AVERSE

How to play: how many can you identify in your office? See page 18 for interpretations

BULLSHIT BINGO – The team talk

COAL FACE	FEEDBACK	WITHIN OUR GIFT	ENERGY LEVELS	SHARE AND AIR	ONE TEAM	HOLDING OUR NERVE	PULL OUT ALL THE STOPS	TICK THE BOXES
WE'RE ALL IN THIS TOGETHER	WHEN THE GOING GETS TOUGH…	FEELS LIKE WE'RE IN THE RIGHT PLACE	GET OUR ACT TOGETHER	THINK OUTSIDE THE BOX	RIDING THE RAZOR BLADE	JUMP THROUGH HOOPS	WAKE UP AND SMELL THE COFFEE	WINDOW
EXPLORE THE OPTIONS	DO YOU READ ME?	COCKS ON THE BLOCK	ACTION	LAST CHANCE SALOON	PUMP UP THE VOLUME	SHIT OR BUST	TALKING SHOP	SHIT HIT THE FAN
GET OUR DUCKS IN A ROW	SIGN OFF	BOILER ROOM	DANCE ROUND YOUR HANDBAGS	RAMP IT UP	WORKING PARTY	BRAINSTORM	VERBAL DIARRHOEA	SAVE OUR BACON
DISSEMINATE	BIG ASK	OBJECTIVE	RATCHET IT UP	HUDDLE	GOING TITS OUT	WORKSHOP	YOU GUYS	RISKS

How to play: simply tick off six words in one meeting and shout out BINGO!

3. War, battles, fighting and guns

"Ah, this is obviously some strange usage of the word 'safe' that I wasn't previously aware of."

Arthur Dent
The Hitchhiker's Guide to the Galaxy
By Douglas Adams

War, battles, fighting, guns

Here is where the fighting style of management takes over and it has to be said that this relatively unsophisticated and robust language is mainly used by men; women tend to use cleverer imagery, sometimes even likening themselves to character's such as Atlanta the Huntress or Boudicca and, surprisingly often, she-wolves.

Thatcher clones and Churchillian managers love taking centre stage when there's a problem to be sorted or a competitor to be taken on, turning a simple marketing plan into a major **field of operations** with **combatants** and the **enemy**. They love to imagine the smell of napalm or cordite filling the air; in reality though it is actually the smell of bullshit.

Battle ground

Meaning – usually referring to the market in which the company is trading.

Bullshit – the place of work, **war zone** is the same as battle ground but it sounds more modern.

Battle royal
Meaning – probably originally from cockfighting though more associated with ultra-violent Japanese films, it means an unusually fierce fight where the contestants have no choice but to fight.
Bullshit – great for those outside looking in, awful for those involved.

Bite the bullet
Meaning – something has to be done and it's painful, from the fact that before anaesthetics, soldiers bit on a bullet to help cope with the pain.
Bullshit – a rare thing for a bullshit merchant to endure, usually there's a fall guy somewhere.

Fall on your sword
Meaning – to take the blame and lose your job in the process.
Bullshit – usually with a nice package.

Going great guns
Meaning – going exceptionally well, apparently this stems from a British naval expression from the 1700s when 'blowing great guns' meant a violent gale.
Bullshit – a lot of hot air in practice.

Going into battle
Meaning – about to start or get involved in a fight.
Bullshit – one mainly used for hostile takeovers, a good euphemism as it implies that the user is tough and up for the fight.

Going nuclear
Meaning – getting out of hand in a big way.
Bullshit – as long as they are not involved, the company bullshitter will be happy…

Grenades
Meaning – unexpected and unforeseen events.
Bullshit – always keep a few handy, just in case.

Hit them where it hurts
Meaning – a competition busting tactic to really do damage to another company.
Bullshit – ouch!

In the armoury/arsenal
Meaning – as in 'have we got anything left in the arsenal?'
Bullshit – usually the answer is no…

In the trenches
Meaning – this is a bit like **battle ground** but involves the troops rather than a boardroom battle.
Bullshit – the implication is that it's a much harder and longer affair.

It's a war out there
Meaning – it's a hostile environment.
Bullshit – a great saying for giving impact but when it's about something like the toy market, well it's just not a war is it, nothing like in fact.

Kamikaze action
Meaning – to do something suicidal, not literally.
Bullshit – something the bullshitter usually likes to watch a colleague or a competitor do.

Keeping your powder dry
Meaning – originally referring to gunpowder, now used primarily regarding keeping something back or not reacting to an initial attack.
Bullshit – everyone keeps something back except the honest, stupid and naïve.

Kill
Meaning – destroy, murder, end.
Bullshit – used by competitive managers or at least those who want to appear competitive, it's mainly used against competitors to 'kill the opposition'; it's the right thing to be heard saying.

Knowing which way the wind blows
Meaning – be aware of what's going on in a fluid situation.
Bullshit – keeping downwind of your quarry is an essential skill of attack-minded bullshitting.

Lead from the front, leading the line
Meaning – to take the initiative, be the first, show strong leadership qualities.
Bullshit – those in front always take the first bullets and are first to tread on the landmines…

Light the blue torch paper
Meaning – start some fireworks.
Bullshit – something bullshitters love to do…

Live by the sword, die by the sword
Meaning – if you live your life aggressively, then there's a high probability that it will end in the same way.
Bullshit – people who act in this way are always amazed when someone stabs them, especially as it's usually in the back.

Lock and load
Meaning – get ready for action.
Bullshit – popularised in everything from John Wayne to Star Trek, it should actually be load and lock, but that's Hollywood for you.

Lock, stock and barrel
Meaning – the whole lot.
Bullshit – originally from all the parts in a flintlock, now more associated with gangsters so people think they sound cool and hard by saying it. Sad.

Loose cannon
Meaning – someone who is unpredictable.
Bullshit – there's nothing more unsettling for senior management than

someone equally senior saying something harmful about the company, albeit with the best intentions; it's great to watch though.

Minefield
Meaning – something littered with problems.
Bullshit – **Tap dancing in a minefield** is a descriptive way of saying 'doing something and avoiding problems along the way'.

Mines, Landmines
Meaning – problems…
Bullshit – another image to conjure with here, managers will look at their plans, talk about how to access the **low hanging fruit**, the **long term aims**, the **short term gains** and then ask if there are any likely landmines on the way; sounds good like they're on the ball and is an excellent bullshit term. Bullshitters love laying them; their nightmare is finding them.

Mission critical
Meaning – vital to the success of the mission.
Bullshit – the main problem being that everything becomes mission critical.

Molotov cocktails
Meaning – more problems but ones to be created for the opposition.
Bullshit – a weapon beloved of the company bullshitter.

On the charge
Meaning – on a roll to victory.
Bullshit – many companies like to believe they're charging to a great victory, sadly most are deluded.

Pre-emptive strike
Meaning – to attack first in anticipation of an attack from the opposition.
Bullshit – not the usual bullshit tactic as it could eventually lead to

potential exposure and possible defeat. One for the gung-ho managers.

Shotgun approach
Meaning – take many different approaches towards the same goal.
Bullshit – chuck enough shit at a wall and some of it will stick.

Take the flak
Meaning – taking the blame or criticism.
Bullshit – usually on behalf of someone who has set you up.

Wagons in a circle
Meaning – from the practice of European settlers, under attack from American Indians, of putting their wagons in a circle to defend themselves from attack.
Bullshit – most people under 30 have no clue what this means, never having seen a John Wayne movie; that won't stop older managers using it though.

Waiting for the cavalry to arrive
Meaning – waiting to be saved.
Bullshit – another Hollywood-derived war term, many companies also have their **wagons in a circle** and are being **surrounded by Indians**; it's a shame these sayings are going out of use really.

Walking wounded
Meaning – those left, bloodied but able to move.
Bullshit – those left after a particularly bloody take-over battle, the poor saps who have to pick up the pieces.

Weapons grade
Meaning – extra strength, extreme.
Bullshit – as in 'you have a weapons grade case there'; can't help thinking that this should be followed by 'Big Boy!'

BULLSHIT BINGO – War

BATTLE GROUND	GREAT GUNS	THE ARSENAL	LEADING THE LINE	LOOSE CANNON	WAGONS IN A CIRCLE
FRONT LINE	BITE THE BULLET	IT'S WAR OUT THERE	TAKING FLAK	LOCK, STOCK AND BARREL	HIT THEM WHERE IT HURTS
MOLOTOV COCKTAILS	FALL ON YOUR SWORD	KEEP YOUR POWDER DRY	SHOTGUN APPROACH	LOCK AND LOAD	GOING NUCLEAR
TIPTOEING THROUGH THE MINEFIELD	SAVED BY THE CAVALRY	WALKING WOUNDED	MISSION CRITICAL	LIVE BY THE SWORD AND DIE BY THE SWORD	TAP DANCING THROUGH A MINEFIELD
LAND MINES	THE ARMORY	LEADING FROM THE FRONT	PRE-EMPTIVE STRIKE	KAMIKAZE	WEAPONS GRADE
MINEFIELD	SMOKING OUT	GRENADES	KILL	ON THE CHARGE	IN THE TRENCHES

How to play: simply tick off six words in one meeting and shout out BINGO!

4. Excuses, disasters and why it all went wrong

"No one is interested until you make a mistake…"

Anonymous

Excuses, disasters and why it all went wrong…

In big business, it's mainly a matter of luck as to whether things work out well, especially in public limited companies where the overwhelming need to offer something positive to shareholders every year prevents long term planning.

Covering their back, setting up scapegoats and having credible excuses to hand is a major part of the company bullshitter's art, and to some, it really is an art form. A few managers have the amazing ability to avoid taking any flak; for observers it's a complete mystery and something that can't help but be admired, but for most it's all about lining up the excuses and keeping their jobs.

Here's a few of the most common terms and excuses, get the violin ready…

20-20 hindsight
Meaning – looking back with perfect clarity.
Bullshit – reviewing mistakes that with 20-20 hindsight look just bleeding obvious.

A bridge too far
Meaning – from the book by Cornelius Ryan and the Richard Attenborough film where the battle for the bridge at Arnhem proved too much for Allied troops to capture.
Bullshit – in this context, it's applied to a company taking too big a risk; using this phase is risky as you could seem negative, so not a good bullshit term.

A rising tide that lifts all boats
Meaning – we're all in this together, in this situation all will become obvious.
Bullshit – usually said by a senior executive when referring to a company-wide issue, the real meaning is that they're in the shit and everyone is going down with them. Often followed up with 'when the tide goes out, all the wrecks are visible', the boss is looking for someone to blame. Interesting that some sources indicate that JFK used this term to the effect that everyone benefits, but we like our version.

Arse saving exercise
Meaning – an attempt to save oneself.
Bullshit – beloved of managers everywhere, the arse saving exercise is standard practice for all those who want to apportion blame elsewhere.

Asking the impossible
Meaning – a request to do an unlikely task or achieve an unattainable goal.
Bullshit – some managers will say 'I'm not asking for the impossible' while knowing they are; they think they'll get better results, but their staff just lose heart.

At the end of the day
Meaning – in the end.
Bullshit – usually said in the context of 'at the end of the day, we have to bloody well do something…' The last few words are said in a high-pitched voice.

Ball juggling

Meaning – to cope with several tasks at once, akin to a juggler juggling several balls in the air.

Bullshit – common habit among inexperienced or nervous male managers who, as they present their latest plan, try to look relaxed by putting a hand in their pocket; the extent of their nervousness or even absentmindedness is given away by how much they play with their testicles, having said that, it's probably the same as *Balls in the air*.

Balls in the air

Meaning – to cope with several tasks at once, akin to a juggler juggling several balls in the air.

Bullshit – some will tell you that management is all about keeping as many balls in the air as possible; it's also about keeping spinning plates spinning and any other multi-tasking imagery you care to name. It's used by those who just want to appear busy, but beware of managers who talk constantly about how big their team is and how much their turnover is, just to impress – with more than six **direct reports**, they are either exceptional or their boss is setting them up to fail.

Between a rock and a hard place

Meaning – caught between two unpalatable solutions.

Bullshit – a staff member is asked to do something that they know is fundamentally wrong but haven't the courage to tell the boss why. They know that if they do as asked and it goes wrong (and they know it will), they'll get the blame but are helpless to prevent it.

Big ask

Meaning – a large request, huge favour or a difficult target.

Bullshit – 'It's a big ask' says your colleague while appearing to suck a lemon. A common tactic in budget negotiations, usually the sign of a desperate effort to reduce targets; watch the body language for collar tugging and chair shifting and you should get an idea of how desperate they really are.

Blamestorm
Meaning – a period after something has gone wrong when blame is being apportioned.
Bullshit – time to watch your back, as managers will be trawling the office to find someone else to blame for their shortcomings and failures.

Blood bath
Meaning – a massacre, a period when there are lots of sackings.
Bullshit – the theory is that by announcing the sackings all at once, all the publicity happens in one go; it may also hide many other issues that the company involved doesn't want to advertise.

Bumpy ride
Meaning – a stormy period for a company, for example, if they are being taken over aggressively or are victims of a fluctuating market.
Bullshit – point to market forces and mention this term several times as a way to cover up shortcomings.

Catch 22
Meaning – from Joseph Heller's outstanding novel *Catch 22*, the premise being that anyone who applied to get out of US military service on the grounds of insanity was behaving rationally and thus couldn't be insane.
Bullshit – it's (usually erroneously) used to describe any number of situations where it seems there's no way out.

Compliance
Meaning – agreeing to a request, doing what's been asked.
Bullshit – a common worry for companies that depend on other companies to sell their products. For example, a manufacturer may buy space in a supermarket chain to promote their latest wonder product, only to find that many stores in the chain don't put the product out. This is poor compliance on behalf of the supermarket chain. It's a great excuse if sales look poor; just get a few photos of crappy displays to back the case.

Deep diving
Meaning – detailed analysis combined with problem solving.
Bullshit – a great bullshitting term used to describe a very detailed investigation of a business, project or situation. 'It's gone wrong; we must do some deep diving to find out why'. People will think you're extra clever for using this one. Some people don't deep dive, they **get granular**.

Disappear up your own backside
Meaning – get so complicated and too convoluted to understand.
Bullshit – when attempting to solve a convoluted problem, you can apparently actually physically disappear up your own backside in an attempt to get an answer.

Enough on my plate
Meaning – too much to do (so they say).
Bullshit – yeah right, lazy git.

Fence mending
Meaning – repairing relationships.
Bullshit – for some reason, this always gets applied to political relationships between countries, but most managers spend their time **mending fences**, **building bridges** and **knocking down barriers**.

Flaky
Meaning – odd, eccentric, loose.
Bullshit – the plan was flaky, execution was flaky, the thinking was flaky – take your pick.

Fluid
Meaning – unclear, unresolved.
Bullshit – one of the great delaying words, the situation is always fluid, anything can happen, best wait until we're sure…and so on.

From day one
Meaning – from the start.
Bullshit – it never worked from day one, but we kept going anyway…

Genie is out of the bottle
Meaning – to let something bad or unwanted happen, this cannot then be stopped.
Bullshit – a nightmare for the company bullshitter, they will go into overdrive attempting to apportion blame elsewhere and minimise their exposure.

Go back to basics
Meaning – going back to fundamental practices, nothing fancy.
Bullshit – a classic when a company has gone through a bad patch and got away from what they are good at, usually heard when new management has arrived and feels the need to sort things out. When this is bandied about, it's probably right to leave, or of course, you could come up with a great solution to save the company.

Hobson's choice
Meaning – a situation in which it seems that there are choices, but there is really only one course of action that you can take. Originally from an English stable owner, Thomas Hobson, who required his customers to take the horse nearest the stable door or none at all.
Bullshit – not much bullshit opportunity but good for excuses as some people don't realise what it means and won't like to admit it.

In the pipeline
Meaning – being planned, on its way.
Bullshit – one of the great excuse phrases, when the work hasn't been done, it's in the pipeline.

Kick ass
Meaning – a severe telling off geared to motivate a team.
Bullshit – American for **a kick up the backside**, it's usually a bollocking done just for effect, so well into the realms of company bullshit.

Knock-on effect
Meaning – an incidental or secondary result.
Bullshit – the after effects of something going wrong can last for some time; a poor manager in a powerful job can cause havoc for years after they have left, while the company bullshitter lives for the ability to savour the effect their actions have on others.

Last chance saloon
Meaning – out of options, near the end.
Bullshit – a favourite of journalists, defeatist managers and realists.

Left hand not knowing what the right hand is doing
Meaning – lack of communication, people acting in a certain way, assuming that colleagues are doing the same.
Bullshit – a classic and a very common occurrence in businesses everywhere.

Less is more
Meaning – make more by doing less.
Bullshit – a true bullshit classic, this is a mantra often repeated by executives who work in a complex business and who don't understand it. There are also those who over complicate everything they do and businesses who try to do too much, so maybe there's something in it after all.

Let's not go there...
Meaning – let's not discuss this topic.
Bullshit – because it's too bloody embarrassing...or too complicated.

Limited bandwidth
Meaning – lack of resources.
Bullshit – when applied to people, it can mean they are too busy or usually by implication that they are just thick.

Lose the plot
Meaning – get badly distracted from the main cause or issue.
Bullshit – when companies lose the plot, it means they're close to **meltdown**, shares are in **free fall** and they're a **basket case**. When people lose it in the office, they're classed as a bit mad...

Naming and shaming
Meaning – highlighting and embarrassing those who have committed an offence or made a mistake.
Bullshit – something the company bullshitter takes great delight in, provided they are not involved.

Nest-guarding
Meaning – keeping information in an attempt to maintain a position of power or to justify a role.
Bullshit – less overt than **empire building**, most managers do this when they feel under threat, which in some companies is most of the time and a major reason why they're not doing well.

Nightmare
Meaning – a bad dream, a horrifying experience.
Bullshit – the stressed and the panicked love this word, but it's particularly beloved by the drama queens who flounce round the office saying 'oh my god, it's a nightmare!' when usually they've just run out of paper clips.

Noise on the line
Meaning – distractions.
Bullshit – Author: 'I've got so much noise on the line I can't finish this book on time.' Publisher: 'Just fucking finish it or the lads will pay a visit.'

Non-core
Meaning – non-essential, not central to the issue.
Bullshit – the first departments to go in a company restructure are

always those where either the manager hasn't fought sufficiently hard for their cause or those that are considered non-core by whoever is responsible for **re-engineering** the business – usually anything creative.

No win situation
Meaning – whatever happens you can't win.
Bullshit – one of the great excuses for the bullshitting manager, usually there's a way out of any situation but it would mean losing face or doing something radical, which means taking a risk.

Off line
Meaning – not publicly, away from the main aims.
Bullshit – this can be used in three ways; firstly as though **off message**, secondly to take an issue away from the public as it may be too embarrassing to air and lastly the broadband has broken half way through a session of Final Fantasy.

Ohnosecond
Meaning – the second that you realise something went badly wrong.
Bullshit – a company bullshitter's nightmare.

Open heart surgery
Meaning – major repairs.
Bullshit – a company needing open heart surgery is in real trouble; of course, new management taking over the stricken beast will always want others to believe it's worse than it really is so that when recovery happens, it looks all the better.

Out of the loop
Meaning – not included.
Bullshit – 'I was out of the loop on this one'; a great 'not me Guv' excuse if ever there was one.

Park it
Meaning – put to one side to be dealt with later.

Bullshit – the province of managers who only want to discuss items on their agenda and nothing else. The parked items are rarely returned to.

Quick fix
Meaning – a running repair, short-term repair.
Bullshit – the quick fix is very common, particularly in those companies listed on the stock exchange that have to justify their actions once a year. It's a symptom of **short-term thinking** and an overwhelming desire to keep shareholders from bad news.

Read the riot act
Meaning – give a serious telling off, after the 1715 Riot Act in England where if a group of more than 12 people didn't disperse after the Riot Act was read to them, they could be legally arrested.
Bullshit – good job it was repealed in 1986, now usually associated with empty threats so not used as often as it once was.

Rearranging the deckchairs on the *Titanic*
Meaning – pointlessly making changes in the face of an impending disaster.
Bullshit – particularly apt for the period just before a company goes into a disastrous trading period, when management desperately applies unworkable remedies in the hope something will save them; others will go about their daily tasks as if nothing were happening.

Review, revisit, re-examine
Meaning – analyse.
Bullshit – this is done usually with **20/20 hindsight**; blame is apportioned and **heads will roll**. Bizarrely, reviews are only carried out when things go badly, not when things are going well.

Risk averse
Meaning – hates taking risks, cowardly by implication, cautious by nature.
Bullshit – frustrating to work with, nothing really gets done without team members taking things into their own hands and taking risks on their manager's behalf.

Risk factors
Meaning – something which increases the risk or likelihood of something going wrong.
Bullshit – the risk averse and cautious manager sees dangers everywhere with the potential to expose them, financial types being the worst pessimists; the company bullshitter will come up with a few they hadn't previously thought of just to wind them up.

Sanity check
Meaning – does it look right, a final check that all is OK.
Bullshit – the top company bullshitter, while slightly insane, will always have checked their work before it goes public.

Save our bacon
Meaning – rescuing a situation.
Bullshit – substitute the 'our' in this phrase for 'my' and you'll be nearer the truth.

Scenario
Meaning – an outline of events.
Bullshit – the scenario is always changing and so how can people ever get it right!

Second hand bullshit
Meaning – repetition of other people's bullshit.
Bullshit – a real crime for the company bullshitter and frustrating for everyone else.

Shambles
Meaning – a complicated mess.
Bullshit – in the company bullshitter's mind, a shambles is what happens when other people get it wrong, when it happens to them; it's a complex and variable situation.

Shit hit the fan
Meaning – a good visual metaphor meaning when something goes wrong it will leave a right mess.
Bullshit – whoever came up with this phrase deserves some sort of medal.

Shit or bust
Meaning – to do or die.
Bullshit – the province of the desperate and the unwise.

Shoot oneself in the foot
Meaning – something that backfires or a mistake that comes back to haunt you.
Bullshit – Schadenfreude is a wonderful thing…

Sign off
Meaning – to conclude, give approval.
Bullshit – standard company bullshitter practice is not to sign anything off without the sign off of their superior, deflecting any potential blame in the process.

Skeletons in the cupboard
Meaning – unknown issues or hidden problems arising.
Bullshit – well, we've all got our little secrets haven't we?

Sledgehammer to crack a nut
Meaning – an over-the-top solution to a small problem.
Bullshit – a common problem in businesses today is where an inordinate amount of time and money goes into solving small prob-

lems and larger issues get ignored. People make a show of problem solving just to get noticed.

Stick to the knitting
Meaning – do the things you are good at, don't try to be too clever.
Bullshit – this is what most companies should do but they get over ambitious or complacent and it all ends in tears...

Sub-optimal
Meaning – below standard.
Bullshit – in some areas of business these days, it's just not right to say that something has been fucked up or performance is rubbish, no, it's sub-optimal – much less confrontational.

Systemic
Meaning – of a whole system or body.
Bullshit – 'I think you'll find the problem is systemic' says the worker, 'Systemic? It's got a fungal infection?' says the boss. Yes this actually happened...see **404**.

Throw in everything including the kitchen sink
Meaning – keep nothing back.
Bullshit – a bit like **Shit or Bust**, it's a bit desperate but common in end of season sales for example.

Throw the baby out with the bath water
Meaning – destroying something good while ridding yourself of something bad.
Bullshit – surprisingly common, especially when new management arrives, keen to make their little mark.

Tick the boxes
Meaning – achieved all the right things, taken from an imaginary checklist.
Bullshit – the province of the arse coverer, the paranoid and the risk averse.

Tits up
Meaning – going wrong.
Bullshit – an enduring image in some circumstances.

TLC
Meaning – tender loving care.
Bullshit – for when things are just a little bit wrong rather than completely fucked, bless.

Took a haircut (took a bath) on that one
Meaning – took a loss.
Bullshit – apparently common parlance in some offices – weird or what?

Vacuum up
Meaning – clear up after the mess, take into account everything missed.
Bullshit – usually the job of some poor sap that's been brought in to sort out something that went wrong.

We're in this together, one team
Meaning – collective responsibility, all take the consequences.
Bullshit – it's all about deflecting blame.

Where to from here?
Meaning – what's the next action?
Bullshit – because I haven't a clue…

BULLSHIT BINGO – Excuses and why it all went wrong…

20-20 HINDSIGHT	NIGHTMARE	FROM DAY ONE	OPEN HEART SURGERY	OUT OF THE LOOP	SANITY CHECK
NO WIN SITUATION	A BRIDGE TOO FAR	FLUID	LIMIT BANDWIDTH	IN THE PIPELINE	SIGN OFF
ARSE SAVING EXERCISE	BACK TO BASICS	DEEP DIVING	FENCE MENDING	KNOCK-ON EFFECT	TICK THE BOXES
A RISING TIDE FLOATS ALL BOATS	BLOOD BATH	LESS IS MORE	ASKING THE IMPOSSIBLE	QUICK FIX	SUB-OPTIMAL
CATCH 22	BALLS IN THE AIR	AT THE END OF THE DAY…	BIG ASK	NONE CORE	SYSTEMIC
NOISE ON THE LINE	BETWEEN A ROCK AND A HARD PLACE	LEFT HAND NOT KNOWING WHAT THE RIGHT IS DOING	REARRANGING THE DECKCHAIRS ON THE *TITANIC*	RISK FACTORS	STICK TO THE KNITTING

How to play: simply tick off six words in one meeting and shout out BINGO!

5. Politics, PR and spin

"The best minds are not in government. If any were, business would hire them away."

Ronald Reagan

Politics, PR and spin

Politics is so rife with clichés, double meanings and media bullshit, alongside the political fakery, that it warrants a whole book devoted to the subject. As we're mostly concerned with office bullshit, we'll content ourselves with a few relevant terms and a couple of bingo cards, one specially designed to get you through a Jeremy Paxman interview.

Most of this book was written during a UK election campaign and it was interesting to draw parallels with the way each of the parties were changing policies and jostling for the voters' attention and the way company bullshitters do the same thing.

PR and spin are all about bullshit, the art of making something appear more positive than it really is and the covering up of wrong doings and passing the buck.

Sadly the real problems get ignored, often because **spin doctors** and politicians are so busy covering their arses and putting over their message that they can't see the most obvious solutions.

Here are a few areas of classic bullshit, clichés and spin...

Bear with me
Meaning – stick with me because I want to say something I think is important…
Bullshit – …and I don't want to answer your question.

Became a politician to make a difference in people's lives
Meaning – a will to do good in the community.
Bullshit – a few hard-working politicians actually do try to do some good; for the majority, it's about power and bullshit.

Big lie
Meaning – a whopper, so large it must be true because no one would dare say it if it wasn't, a trick inherited from the Nazis and Dr Joseph Goebbels who said, 'If you tell a lie big enough and keep repeating it, people will eventually come to believe it.'
Bullshit – amazingly people still actually try this one…and people still fall for it.

Categorical denial
Meaning – a complete rebuttal of the accusation.
Bullshit – generally if someone offers up a categorical denial, they're hoping that by being firm about it the problem will go away; sadly for them, it usually doesn't.

Demonstrated real leadership
Meaning – shown that they're not as weak as everyone thought.
Bullshit – this is usually done with the connivance of a sympathetic media until they get bored and support someone else.

Dog-whistle politics
Meaning – a term originating in Australia, it is the pushing of subliminal messages in speeches and using specific language that would only be picked by targeted sections of the electorate; like a dog whistle, it's only audible to whom it's aimed.
Bullshit – so many examples, it's hard to know where to start but one

of the most obvious would be a politician demonstrating commitment to one cause that offers a beneficial **halo effect**, enabling other less popular policies to be more palatable. For example, George Bush, by extolling the virtues of God and patriotism, it enables him to get policies past the electorate that they would normally be against had a non-believer touted them.

Doing a Jo Moore

Meaning – attempting to release bad news when something else is happening that is very big and unrelated and then being caught doing it. Jo Moore was a civil servant who suggested it would be a good idea to release some controversial announcements [about councillors' allowances] as the World Trade Center was being attacked, in the hope that they would subsequently be ignored in the furore surrounding that disaster.

Bullshit – to her credit, Moore apologised for her actions and is no longer a civil servant, but it only really served to highlight how much **spin** and bullshit there has been in UK government.

Expectations

Meaning – anticipation of a result, usually something good.

Bullshit – bullshitting is largely about managing people's expectations, so simply delivering what was previously thought undeliverable.

Focus on the issues, not personalities

Meaning – not insulting the opposition but concentrating on policies and what is actually going to get done.

Bullshit – politicians always say they're going to do this but never do, it's always easier to be destructive than constructive and it gets better headlines.

Grass roots

Meaning – local, common people.

Bullshit – a patronising term to describe what goes on at the level of politics where people do the real work. Sometimes they rise up and do something at a national level, like get rid of the leader, always a pleasure.

Just let me finish
Meaning – usually said while being interrupted and when the politician wants to make a point, no matter what anyone else thinks.
Bullshit – very common in British political talk and radio shows...

Knows what the country needs, do what's right for Britain
Meaning – showing a fundamental knowledge of what is good for the country.
Bullshit – by implication, strong leadership against strong opposition from nasty foreign types.

Laying the foundations
Meaning – starting something, something by implication.
Bullshit – politicians never start anything, they lay the foundations, **prepare the ground** and generally imply things are much more important than they really are.

Mandate
Meaning – authority to do something.
Bullshit – these days, often applied to the size of a government's majority; the bigger the majority; the bigger the mandate. It doesn't actually mean that when a government gets in power with a strong mandate, they'll actually do what they said they would do in order to get that mandate.

Man of the people
Meaning – has an understanding of what people are looking for from a leader, a good bloke with working class values and credentials. It's a term rarely applied to women.
Bullshit – a difficult thing to achieve as it can be perceived as disingenuous or patronising; most politicians are pretending to understand what the people want, usually based on polls, the media and market research.

Moral high ground
Meaning – a position of strength dictated by the virtuous superiority of one person's position over another.
Bullshit – one of the key arts of bullshitting is to gain the moral high ground, especially when one has no right to be there.

Neocon
Meaning – Short for neo-conservative, the most conspicuous policy is probably hard line conservative values allied to aggressive foreign policies.
Bullshit – this is allied to an extensive taking of the moral high ground and the use of dog whistle politics.

Open government
Meaning – government where the workings are visible.
Bullshit – an attempt by New Labour to make government more transparent, which worked until it became transparent to them that it might embarrass them sometimes.

Ordinary, decent, hardworking people
Meaning – the common man, normal people.
Bullshit – often used by a senior government person or MP to give the electorate the impression that they're on their side, they're not of course.

Our children's future is at stake
Meaning – by implication, storing up trouble for future generations.
Bullshit – tugging at the heartstrings here, after all, who would want to hurt the poor little kiddie-widdies? Often said by opposition parties, watch out for u-turns once in power.

Polls and statistics
Politics, polls and statistics go hand in hand and everyone was amazed when the polls on the BBC at the last election actually got it right. Essentially, the trick is to quote figures that put the speaker's party in

good light or trash the opposition's policies, and then repeat the statistics (even if they're wrong or dubious) as often as possible.

Smoking gun
Meaning – indisputable evidence.
Bullshit – there's no smoking gun in the Whitehouse, Number 10 or the MD's office, it's somewhere else...honest guv.

Spin
Meaning – the process of putting something in a positive light.
Bullshit – bullshit.

Taken out of context
Meaning – words lifted from something said or written but given a meaning not meant by the originator.
Bullshit – politicians are always being either misquoted or having words put into their mouths, it's a sure sign of backtracking...

Teflon
Meaning – non-stick chemical.
Bullshit – whether a Teflon politician or a manager, they never seem to get into trouble when something they are responsible for goes wrong.

We have to look to the future
Meaning – prepare, be prepared.
Bullshit – in other words, wait until we get into power then we can change everything.

Will of the people
Meaning – what the electorate wants.
Bullshit – what we want the electorate to think they want.

With respect
Meaning – I'm sorry but...

Bullshit – when people say 'with respect', they in fact mean the opposite.

Wizard of Oz
Meaning – 1939 Oscar winning fantasy film.
Bullshit – when they run out of ideas, political commentators get desperate and start comparing politicians to Tin Men, Cowardly Lion's, Wicked Witches and Dorothy.

Top tips on how to be a successful politician
1. Always dress smartly, unless it's good spin to be seen casually dressed, for example, on the presidential ranch.
2. Never give a straight answer; if you have to, then make sure there are plenty of caveats and a get out clause.
3. Believe your own lies; a lack of conscience always helps, as does an ability to pretend you care.
4. Never apologise, unless it puts you in a good light.
5. Be completely unembarrassed about maintaining double standards.
6. Be aware of the previous policies of your competition, they will be useful.
7. Extol Victorian values and virtues but only if you're fairly virtuous; if not, then make sure you have a good lawyer.
8. Become religious but not too religious.
9. Ensure you get good media training. When interviewed, learn the art of deflection; when asked a question, reply in such a way that you put over the points that you want to talk about.
10. Never take responsibility for anything, be ambiguous.
11. Cultivate the ability to turn unpopular actions into heroism.
12. Take advantage of every legal freebie you can.
13. If you are male, ensure that your wife (you must be married) is attractive but not so attractive that she takes attention away from you. Never become the golden couple.
14. If you are female, ensure that your husband is anonymous, particularly if you are attractive. Never become a golden couple.

15. Keep your children away from the media.
16. Never become too associated with a single cause unless you are happy to be sidelined.
17. Don't be too bland, smarmy, clever, unpleasant, irascible, old fashioned or too trendy (especially if you're over 40).
18. Choose a car that isn't too flash but not too sensible; ensure that the brand is right and not too foreign.
19. Be seen to recycle.
20. Always have a fall back position or at least a fall guy to take the blame.
21. If you don't think you can do any of the above, then just tell the truth and the hell with it.

Here, instead of a political bingo card, we thought it a good idea to honour Jeremy Paxman, whose interview style has become something of a legend and an institution.

BULLSHIT BINGO – Paxman interview

I ASK YOU AGAIN	BEAR WITH ME	HOW MUCH?	SO YOU'RE SAYING THAT XXX WAS WRONG?	DESPITE THE FACT THAT...	LET'S LOOK AT...
I'VE ALREADY ANSWERED THAT QUESTION	REAL LEADERSHIP	WELL I WOULD ANSWER BUT YOU KEEP INTERRUPTING	YOU ARE ABSOLUTELY CONFIDENT OF THAT ARE YOU?	DO YOU ACCEPT ANY RESPONSIBILITY?	YOU HAVE ABSOLUTELY NO IDEA HAVE YOU?
COME ON!	JUST ANSWER THE QUESTION...	YOUR POINT IS WHAT?	IN YOUR MANIFESTO IT SAYS QUITE CLEARLY...	THERE'S NO EXCUSE IS THERE?	CAN WE JUST BE CLEAR...
WITH RESPECT	BUT YOU SAID...	YOU DON'T KNOW?	IS THAT PARTY POLICY?	WELL?	YES OR NO?
PLEASE LET ME FINISH	REALLY?	DO YOU SUBSCRIBE TO THAT VIEW?	SO THAT'S A NO THEN?	GIVE US A FIGURE	IS THAT REAL OR JUST MADE UP?
THE POINT HERE IS...	ARE YOU BEING ENTIRELY FRANK?	SO IN SUMMARY...	SO THAT'S A YES IS IT?	DESPITE EVIDENCE TO THE CONTRARY	DO YOU ACCEPT THAT?

How to play: simply tick off six words in one meeting and shout out BINGO!

6. Business guru speak

"The 'Inside-Out' approach to personal and self; even more fundamentally, to start with the most inside part of self – with your paradigms, your character, and your motives. The inside-out approach says that private victories precede public victories, that making and keeping promises to ourselves precedes making and keeping promises to others. It says it is futile to put personality ahead of character, to try to improve relationships with others before improving ourselves."

Steven Covey

Business guru speak

A business guru is someone who makes a pile of money out of telling people how to run a business, usually in an exotic, interesting and original way. Often there's nothing new on offer and what they say is just common sense repackaged as a form of entertainment. Many will earn fortunes appearing at company conferences, holding seminars and of course from the obligatory business book.

Some combine quasi-religious and strong motivational techniques with the sort of language this book is devoted to, and whether they know it or not, they are the inventors of much of the bullshit we find in offices today. It may not be their fault as some of the fools who use their words have no clue what they mean, they just think they sound good.

How to be a business guru...

1. You must have a track record in business, or at least be able to fake one.
2. You should look good in a suit and have the ability to talk loudly. Alternatively, come over as humble, as though you have discovered this great thing and want to share it with the world.
3. Great presentational skills are an absolute must. Rely on religious zeal and shouting if all else fails.
4. It helps if you are American or can put on a great US accent, preferably a New York one. Having a Scottish accent is a good back up, but if you're from Birmingham, forget it.
5. Find an angle, something you can pedal as your own; if in doubt, steal someone else's ideas and repackage them as your own using different words.
6. Publish a book. It has to have a wacky title such as *'How red are your toenails?'* or *'The man who mistook his company for a vibrator'* or an aggressive title like *'Losing is for suckers you sucker'*. The book must be expensive and contain lots of charts, diagrams and illustrations; big font size is also useful if you haven't got much to say.
7. Hire a good PR company to start the media circus rolling.
8. Find an audience.

Guru words and phrases

The guru is a rare breed. He or she will inspire most bullshitters though and here are some of the best phrases that have stemmed from the guru's works.

Action

Meaning – to do something, the general cry is 'who is going to action this?' instead of 'who is going to do this?'

Bullshit – applying words slightly differently to their original use is a feature of business bullshit. The word 'action' sounds a much better word to use in this context as it implies professionalism, a 'can do' attitude and the user sounds more of a leader.

Always on
Meaning – ever alert, ready for action.
Bullshit – 'Imagine that executive' says the guru, 'eyes bright, expression expectant, suited, positive body language, committed, ready for business...he's always on and you should be too' says the guru. 'Sod off mate' thinks the audience.

Barriers
Meaning – something or someone who gets in the way.
Bullshit – gurus love talking about barriers as a non-aggressive term applied to people who don't agree with the objective in hand. 'Breaking down the barriers' generally means pushing through something at the expense of others. Bullshitters use the term to describe someone who is in their way; it's less threatening than 'they should be sacked' but that's what the bullshitter implies by it.

Big picture
Meaning – the wider view, the whole thing.
Bullshit – management will say 'you're not getting the bigger picture', especially when their instructions seem insane, implying that they are somehow aware of facts that you're not, or that the point you're making is so trivial that it's meaningless to someone as important as them. The guru uses the same principle to befuddle the people they are 'training' too.

Call to action
Meaning – an encouragement or inducement to do something.
Bullshit – the guru will say that his or her session is a 'call to action'; in reality, it's a symptom of a desperate management who need something to happen to save them or their company. Usually in response to some event like a poor sales period, the 'call to action' will go out to employees who will be expected to work their asses off to save the day. A great bullshit term as, by implication, the 'caller' is not the one who does the work, that's why it's so popular with gurus.

Catalyst

Meaning – to make something happen without apparent involvement or to be changed by the event that is precipitated.

Bullshit – to make something happen without doing any work. A **catalyst team** is a group of people who rather than do the work, make something happen or force a change in a company. Usually called into action when a company is stagnant, in trouble or running out of ideas. If you hear of such a team being formed in your company, it's probably the right time to **get your coat**.

Closure

Meaning – finished, ended.

Bullshit – achieving closure on a sale or a project is something guru's love, especially good fun is to talk in detail about the path to closure or the journey.

Competitive advantage

Meaning – business guru Michael Porter identified two types of competitive advantage. First, 'cost advantage' where the company delivers the same benefits but at lower cost; second, 'differentiation' where benefits are delivered that exceed those of your competitors.

Bullshit – the third advantage is the *bullshit advantage*, where whichever company lies best about cost savings and benefits is the winner.

Constant change

Meaning – that business is always changing and a good company is always prepared for it. Gurus will point out that change is good and inevitable.

Bullshit – managers are threatened by change, they like their perks and hate a fluid situation. Many will change things just for the sake of it, not really knowing why, just knowing that they have to do something.

Continuous improvement
Meaning – an ongoing commitment to get better both as company and individual.
Bullshit – at least one guru advocates this as a policy and it's been used by many an MD as an excuse for changing their business.

Conversation
Meaning – a spoken exchange.
Bullshit – a favourite of business gurus who talk about having 'conversations' with customers and colleagues in an attempt to avert conflict or provide something positive where often there is nothing of the sort. It's forced and can be a little creepy when a colleague asks to have a 'conversation' with you, especially if they mime quote marks as they say the word. Run!

Customer value
Meaning – providing something extra for customers as a company priority.
Bullshit – good policy but the **bottom line** is always king.

Disconnect
Meaning – a communications breakdown.
Bullshit – a guru's nightmare, as happens when something goes wrong because policy hasn't been well communicated or a team leader hasn't let his team know what's required. Nobody says 'we haven't communicated properly', instead, in the world of business, bullshit people say 'there's been a disconnect'. It's another good example of a word's usage being distorted in the workplace.

Empower
Meaning – give someone the power to do something.
Bullshit – a watchword of a few years ago when business gurus were telling company bosses to empower their staff and 'awaken the giant within'; it's not much used nowadays as management have realised that empowering staff is a very dangerous thing to do.

Energy
On please! The worst bullshit word in the world; anyone using it, saying they need it, saying you need it, saying the company needs it, needs to be punished, very severely. It is almost guaranteed that the user will invoke the opposite reaction to the one envisaged by them.

Engage
Meaning – we need to 'engage' our customers, 'engage' our team-mates, you can't just talk to someone, you need to 'engage' them in a **conversation**; that's how things get done.
Bullshit – a classic example of a guru telling us what we already know, then regurgitating it into something that looks new.

Excellence
Meaning – very good and extremely high standards.
Bullshit – another word that was bandied about in the 1990s, usually along the lines of 'a passion for excellence' or a 'centre of excellence'. These days it seems to have been replaced by terms like **dog's bollocks, off the scale** and **outstanding**.

First principles
Meaning – the initial rules.
Bullshit – whenever the manager starts a project, they always **lay foundations** or establish the **ground rules**; it's a much more important thing to do than to just start something.

Focus
Meaning – a centre of attention or activity, **in the spotlight, under the lens.**
Bullshit – another classic, nearly all managers have used the word mainly when they think their teams have **taken their eyes off the ball.** You'll hear of being customer focused, team focused, client focused, career focused and on and on, well this book is bullshit focused and the word should be banned.

Framework

Meaning – a structure around which a business plan or team is based.

Bullshit – a word lumped together with **template** and **structure**, managers need something to build their plans with and no matter how loose the framework, it is always trotted out as something to **hang things on**. Managers able to work in a fluid situation are viewed with suspicion by others, especially the company bullshitter who tends to need a rigid structure to climb up.

Future facing

Meaning – always looking forward, always planning the future.

Bullshit – gurus will tell companies to learn from the past but not emulate it; they must, above all, be future facing. So don't do what those tossers did in the 1990s; take on the buggers who are trying to grind you down now and identify those who could shaft you in the future and get 'em.

Go for it

This has to be lumped together with **energy** as one of those terms that when someone says 'go for it', accompanied by a punch in the air, the automatic reaction in most people is to do the opposite. It's had its day and the user is a little out of touch, even **kicking ass, pumping up the volume** and **cooking with gas** is out, especially accompanied by **high-fives**. The modern bullshitter has more subtle methods to **rally the troops.**

Hardwire

Meaning – to make something automatic, an integral part of the business.

Bullshit – the guru will give guidance, a strategy will be formed, policies will be made and a new way forward will be created for the company concerned. The new strategy and policies will become part of the company's culture and it will be hardwired in so that you don't bloody well forget it.

Hedgehog concept
Meaning – the hedgehog concept is created by a person working on their own, independently, who can change a company for the better and enhance that person's career in the process. While it stems from an essay written in the 1950s, many gurus have developed the ideology to encourage it.
Bullshit – the company bullshitter's nightmare...

Helicopter vision
Meaning – imagine a managing director 'hovering' over the business, watching events as they happen and taking action accordingly.
Bullshit – great but bear in mind that this could turn into **Seagull vision** where the said manager flies over his staff, makes a loud noise and a great deal of commotion, shits on them occasionally, then takes off when the going gets tough.

Human factor
Meaning – human contribution – good or bad.
Bullshit – no matter how good the plans, there's always someone there who can bollocks it up.

If you keep doing the same thing, the same thing will happen
Well, duh!

Innovation
Meaning – something new and original.
Bullshit – senior managers will often call for innovation in their company, although few know what that means and when something innovative really occurs, they often resist it as it means a change in the status-quo, something which they are very suspicious and wary of. The company bullshitter will never innovate; this would leave them too exposed, although they will happily steal the innovations of others and represent them as their own if it's in their interests.

Joined up thinking
Meaning – when people have separate **conversations**, there are lots of ideas being created and the process of gathering those ideas together to form a plan is called joined up thinking.
Bullshit – this is the sort of term that readily spouts from the mouths of gurus, just talk to people OK...

Lateral thinking
Meaning – an unorthodox approach to problem solving, from the work of the likes of Edward De Bono, lateral thinking is the process of problem solving by looking at the issue in a different way from the usual process.
Bullshit – so you have to **brainstorm, blue sky, think outside the box, stretch the envelope, get granular** and go **deep diving** then.

Leading edge
Meaning – in the vanguard, the foremost in the market.
Bullshit – type 'leading edge' into Google and 31 million responses appear. Gurus have for years encouraged companies to be one step ahead of their competition, to be **future facing, innovative** and to **lead the market**. Obviously, some companies are claiming to be leading edge when they clearly aren't, so is the real thing corporate bullshit or self delusion?

Make it happen
Meaning – do it, get it done.
Bullshit – gurus encourage managers to **get things done** and to be more **task oriented**, making things happen can become an obsession leading to stress, over work and efficiency – whatever next...

Making a difference
Meaning – change things, for good by implication.
Bullshit – young managers are often told to make a mark, but to the horror of most senior managers, gurus want them to actually make a

difference; this is seen as threatening and unhealthy as it could really change things.

Mission statement
A true classic, here's one for this book:

The purpose of this book is to highlight the use of bullshit in business and in other walks of life, with the aim of exposing and revealing fakes and bullshitters to the uninitiated, in a humorous and interesting way.

Virtually every large business has a mission statement in some form or another, basically to describe the purpose of the business; it's becoming unfashionable now as a term, replaced by **constitutions**, **manifestos** and **articles**, in other words, more bullshit.

Missionwear is clothing, stationery or anything that has the mission statement printed on it.

Orchestra model
Meaning – a scenario where the leader gives directions tailored to specific groups within the business.
Bullshit – something many gurus bang on about when talking about management structures, it replaces the military based hierarchy we're used to, but it could be efficient and that's the scary thing about it.

Passion
Meaning – excitement, eagerness, boundless enthusiasm.
Bullshit – anyone who tells you that they're passionate about paper clips, widgets, spreadsheets, paperwork or anything remotely boring is lying or mad.

Proactive, Not reactive
Meaning – this is to anticipate and act with forethought instead of waiting for something to happen before taking action.
Bullshit – one of many phrases used as a mantra by company senior

management; usually it's a sign that something has already happened and it's all too late…

Pushing the envelope/Stretch the envelope
Meaning – the theory is that the envelope in question is a technical term relating to the performance of fighter aircraft, with the envelope being the limits of their technical abilities.
Bullshit – a pretty odd way of saying 'how can we do more?'

Raving Fans
Meaning – from a book by Kenneth Blanchard and Sheldon Bowles, a raving fan is a customer who is so overwhelmed by high levels of customer service, so much so that they brag about it and become part of the company 'sales force'.
Bullshit – excellent opportunities for bullshitters; customers like this are also the most gullible as it takes a lot to shift their view if bad service sets in.

Reality check
Meaning – an assessment to determine if the circumstances or expectations conform to what's happening in real life.
Bullshit – for many companies, the real world is something that happens outside of the bubble in which they place themselves, and it can come as a big shock when something that they're convinced is right, turns out to be totally wrong.

Re-engineering
Meaning – this is the examination and then the modification of a company to change it for the better, including the implementation of the changes.
Bullshit – change is always difficult; it means job losses, upheaval, a difficult period all round, though company leaders can't actually say that; much better to re-engineer – it sounds much more professional.

Reinventing

Meaning – a makeover, change back but with a new form, the saying 'we don't need to **reinvent the wheel**' is a common cry among people who resist change or don't want to spend money on change.

Bullshit – this word appears in many guises; companies will be advised by gurus to reinvent themselves after something's gone wrong in order to present a new image, the company bullshitter does it every time they change jobs.

Results driven, outcome driven

Meaning – towards a specific outcome, by implication this is done with high levels of concentration.

Bullshit – this creates a culture dominated by insensitive, single minded shits, you have been warned...

Rules of engagement

Meaning – companies are advised to understand what the rules of engagement are before entering into negotiations, a trading period or a new market.

Bullshit – companies have a tendency not to bother to find out what the parameters are before going **into battle**, which leaves others to clear up the mess.

Step change

Meaning – a radical change, increase in pace.

Bullshit – companies in trouble always talk about making step changes, really what this means is that they're desperately looking for a **magic bullet** or **pot of gold** that could get them out of trouble.

Synergy

Meaning – cooperative interaction among the departments or merged parts of a company, which creates something stronger and works to better effect.

Bullshit – one of the classic business guru words, forgetting the **human factor**, they dream of organisations, corporations and governments working in harmony to solve problems; with synergy, world famine could be eradicated, disease wiped out, war banished and global warming a thing of the past...nice thought though.

Theology
There have been many attempts to ally business culture to religious theology; one of the worst and probably most common is over emphasis on Good versus Evil. One guru once asked 'do you have any colleagues who are truly evil? Is there anything you can do about it?' Bullshitters beware!

The Seven Habits...
Mentioned often by managers who want to impress, from the book *The Seven Habits of Highly Effective People* by Stephen Covey, they are...
1. Be proactive
2. Begin with the end in mind
3. Put first things first
4. Think win-win
5. Seek first to understand, and then be understood
6. Synergize
7. Sharpen the saw

It may appear to be jargonised mumbo-jumbo to some, but they've sold some ten million copies so there must be something in it. It is probably the most shown off book in the office and without even reading or understanding it, people will quote from it, have it on their desk or on display somewhere just to look good. Woe betide any bullshitter who has a boss that has read and understood it...

This leads us neatly on to the bullshitter's bookshelf...

The bullshitter's bookshelf
Looking good, giving the impression that they are up on all the latest management techniques and boning up on all the latest buzzwords,

the accomplished corporate bullshitter will have the appropriate books dotted around their desk. Most business gurus and experts who write their ideas down mean well and some have something genuinely interesting and innovative to say, but when you're out to impress, for the bullshitter, it's about being seen with the right books, whether they understand them or not.

Here are the top ten most common books you'll find on a bullshitter's desk...

1. *Seven Habits of Highly Effective People* by Stephen Covey (see page 89)
   For those times when you really want to confuse your boss.
2. *How to Win Friends and Influence People* by Dale Carnegie
   Top tips on how to get your own way.
3. *The One Minute Manager* by Kenneth Blanchard and Spencer Johnson
   Bought by people who think management is easy.
4. *Who Moved My Cheese?* by Spencer Johnson
   For those who want to pretend that they embrace change.
5. *Winning* by Jack Welsh
   How it should be done...
6. *Getting Things Done* by David Allen
   A bullshitter's nightmare because it actually shows how to do things properly.
7. *Fish!* by Harry Paul, Stephen Lundin and John Christensen
   An uplifting and much quoted parable about fishmongers...it's very short.
8. *Emotional Intelligence* by Daniel Goleman
   One of the best, most popular and least read books.
9. *Art of War* by Sun Tzu
   The one to be seen with...
10. *Feel the Fear and Do It Anyway* by Susan Jeffers
    The one they really read and then hide away...

BULLSHIT BINGO – *Guru speak*

PASSION	ABANDONMENT	ENGAGE	PROACTIVE	RE-ENGINEERING	JOINED UP THINKING	RULES...	ENERGY
DISCONNECT	EXCELLENCE	ALWAYS ON	EMPOWER	MAKE IT HAPPEN	CLOSURE	FIRST PRINCIPLES	COMPETITIVE ADVANTAGE
CLOSURE	HARDWIRE	FRAMEWORK	BIG PICTURE	CHANGE	LEADING EDGE	CONTINUOUS IMPROVEMENT	GETTING THINGS DONE
FOCUS	CATALYST	CONNECT	VISION	INNOVATION	LATERAL THINKING	DRIVEN	MANIFESTO
REALITY CHECK	FUTURE FACING	DISCONNECT	MISSION	MAKE A DIFFERENCE	REINVENTING	STEP CHANGE	THE ENVELOPE
VALUES	SYNERGY	THEOLOGY	FEAR	LATERAL THINKING	CONVERSATION	HUMAN	HARDWIRE

How to play: simply tick off six words in one meeting and shout out BINGO!

7. Consultant bullshit

"A businessman and a consultant had a meeting; the businessman asked what the consultant's rates would be for the suggested project.

'We structure the project up front, and charge £500 initially, for three questions,' replied the consultant.

'Isn't that awfully steep?' asked the businessman.

'Yes, it is,' the consultant replied, 'and what was your third question?'"

Consultant bullshit

Consultants can bullshit with the best of them, there are plenty of words in this book commonly used by them, but here are a few that they really popularised.

Charts, diagrams and anything whizzy is added to presentations and pitches in order to get attention, to liven things up and to give the impression that more work has been done than the reality.

Dog and pony show

Meaning – an over-the-top presentation.

Bullshit – in other words the usual PowerPoint presentation with the usual bullshit.

Holistic

Meaning – taking in the whole picture.

Bullshit – a classic bit of consultant bullshit, talking about taking a holistic approach, encompassing all aspects because that will give the

best results. It will also take the most time and make them more
money as a consequence.

Put flesh on the bones
Meaning – add more detail.
Bullshit – consultants just love this request as it allows them to pad
their work out to make it last longer and appear more authoritative,
earning more cash in the process.

Scope, scoping the opportunity
Meaning – range, size.
Bullshit – the bigger the scope of the job, the bigger the contract.

Squaring the circle
Meaning – trying to do the impossible.
Bullshit – sometimes people use **circling the square**, either way it's
pretty damn confusing.

PowerPoint is the main tool of bullshit for the consultant, and of
course any worth their salt would include a chart within their
presentation. Here are the most common, all designed to impress…

The Boston box

Developed by the Boston consultancy group, this classic device always goes a long way to impress a potential client. Officially known as the Growth-Share matrix, it evaluates a company's products by share and growth potential.

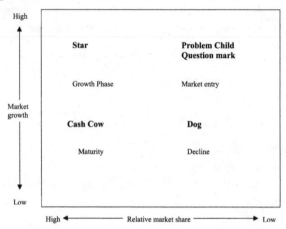

Pie charts

Another bullshit presentation classic, a way of showing portions and ratios.

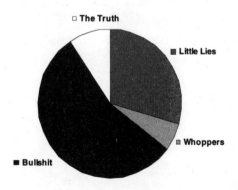

SWOT analysis

It has to be done at the beginning of any bit of company analysis; you can bet it will end up geared so that the consultant will get lots of work out of it.

Strengths | **Weaknesses**

You can sound more important than you are

Make things sound better than they really are

Get yourself out of trouble, get away with things.

Over use can threaten your credibility

Success dependent on strong acting skills, fake sincerity and a good memory for lies

Improved career opportunities

More money, more sex, more success

The truth

Being found out and exposed as a liar

Being undermined by someone who is actually good at their job

Opportunities | **Threats**

Venn diagram

Great for comparisons and finding out what things have in common.

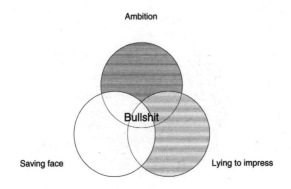

8. Marketing and Advertising

"Me? In love with a pig? Wait 'til I tell the guys in marketing."
Kermit the Frog
The Muppets take Manhattan (1984)

Marketing and Advertising

Here are the major areas in business that are rife with bullshit and general up-its-own-arse nonsense, the difference being that mostly people working in this area actually believe what they're saying without knowing it's bullshit. To the accomplished bullshitter, this is a world in which to shine, lovers of jargon and users of the silky tongue will shine.

Strategy
Many managing directors set the **strategy** themselves; others employ a strategy director whose only role appears to be to organise the company conference where other people's work is delivered, often reworked as their own.

Marketing directors often set strategy, based on **market research**, employing specialist companies and legions of consultants to tell them about their company and **the market** they're working in. Usually any longstanding employee will know as much.

Armed with this information, the company strategy will be formed, but not after lots of the following bullshit.

Acorns, seeds
Meaning – ideas, especially new ones.
Bullshit – there are no new ideas, only those that are approved of.

Blue sky thinking
Meaning – an attempt to tackle an issue or come up with a new strategy or approach by thinking differently, without boundaries and constraints.
Bullshit – if only that were really true…

Brainstorm
Meaning – a meeting where free and original thought is encouraged to solve a problem or to come up with something like a strategy; in less aggressive companies it's also known as a **thought shower**, bless them.
Bullshit – usually the outcome has already been agreed before the meeting and the brainstorm is used to **rubber stamp** the idea.

Customer offer vision
Meaning – the idea of a new company offering to the customer, what it means and what it could be.
Bullshit – one from a company this author once worked for. The MD came up with this to describe her view of what customers wanted. This was followed by the 'Founder Letter' and the creation of a 'Hothouse' and such roles as the 'Change Manager'; a year or so later, the company's sales and shares went into free fall.

Journey
Meaning – moving from one point to the next.
Bullshit – touchy feely types just love talking about the company going on a journey, the **rocky road**, the **bumpy ride** and the **road ahead**. Pass the travel sickness pills.

Strategy
The word strategy covers a multitude of sins and here are just a few of them…

Strategic direction – where we think we're going
Strategic approach – how we think we're going to go about it
Strategic fit – those who are going with us
Strategic goals – what we think we're going to get
Strategic plan – how we think we're going to get there
Strategic thinking – real issues aside, how can we make ourselves look good?

There are various types of strategy:

High risk strategy – don't blame us if it goes wrong
Low risk strategy – it won't go wrong
Exit strategy – for when it does all go wrong
Development strategy – we think we know what to do but we'll take it slowly in case it's wrong, common in government this one
Short term strategy – get it done before we get fired, for most listed companies, this is a way of life
Long term strategy – there's no hurry, by the time anything is implemented the whole situation will have changed anyway

Here's a classic from the UK government's own Strategy Survival Guide:

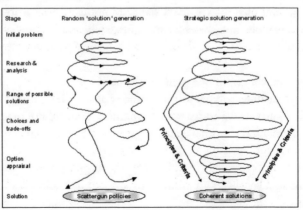

Visioning
Meaning – an essential part of **Strategic thinking**, looking forward to the future, trying to envision what it will be…
Bullshit – look back at previous plans and see where it's got them.

Customers, clients and consumers
Part of any strategy works on, anticipating the future needs and demands of customers; the people who its said employees ultimately work for. Companies will convince themselves that they're offering the ultimate customer service and here are a few of the phrases bandied about.

Client focused
Meaning – a process mainly used in the business-to-business world (**B2B**) where a company delivers new products and services to their clients based on a thorough understanding of their actual needs.
Bullshit – yeah right, sounds good though. See also *Consumer facing*.

Connect
Meaning – to talk, make contact.
Bullshit – 'We must *connect* with our customers' or 'I'm not feeling any connection with you' are terms generally used by people who have no clue how to communicate properly and are usually mystified by the fact that others don't agree with their point of view. Using the word in conversation signifies the most desperate and least socially adjusted of your colleagues. They are to be avoided, disconnected in fact.

Consumer agenda
Meaning – what the customer wants, what they plan to buy.
Predicting what's on their consumers' agendas is for most companies their main preoccupation.
Bullshit – many careers are built by people who manage to kid their colleagues and bosses that they know what customers want. A classic consultant's term.

Consumer facing
Meaning – a company is consumer facing when it works in direct contact with its customers, being aware of their needs and delivering a particular service; many websites are considered 'consumer facing'.
Bullshit – who the hell are they kidding? Many companies will convince themselves they are consumer facing when in fact they are profit facing. See also *Client focused*.

Consumer intuitive
Meaning – being instinctively aware of what your customer wants instinctively without thought.
Bullshit – if you can achieve this, you're a bloody genius and you won't need to bullshit at all.

Customer obsessed
Meaning – knowing about customers' needs and likely requirements to the point of obsession.
Bullshit – companies will say they are customer or consumer obsessed and talk about giving them what they want. In reality, all companies are out to make a profit and will always hold something back. What this really means is giving customers as much as we can get away with so that they give us more of their money than our competitors.

Educating customers
Meaning – persuading customers to part with their cash is an industry in itself and many companies spend fortunes on consultants and business gurus to get the secret to success. Some firms will attempt to change their customers' habits by using techniques such as incentives, a variety of TV channels and advertising, in other words **changing customer behaviour** to their advantage.
Bullshit – customers are stupid; they are only there to be taken advantage of, to further enhance careers.

Empathy
Meaning – being on the customer's side, being aware of their needs in a sympathetic and thoughtful way.
Bullshit – in this context, it's about companies faking empathy with the customer, so that they become loyal spenders, leading to bigger profits and more bullshit.

Top of mind
Meaning – high priority, the product most people think of first in a given situation.
Bullshit – a sort of nirvana for most companies when they can prove that their products are the first for consumers, it's staying there that's the problem and that's when the bullshit kicks in.

Advertising and promotion
No other area in business attracts more bullshit and bullshitters than this, but most fakes are out for themselves and will be treating customers and colleagues with the usual disguised contempt. They will go on about the **four Ps** (price, place, product, and promotion), but much of what's suggested will be advertising **puffery**, in other words, just subjective opinions and superlatives.

So here are the key bullshit words; make sure you stay **on message** with these, the company bullshitter will be **well up to speed**…

All singing, all dancing, Bells and whistles
Meaning – it does everything.
Bullshit – it (the deal or product) comes with everything included and more. Whoever says this is usually keeping something back; be suspicious.

Call to action
Meaning – an encouragement or inducement to do something such as respond to an advert or click on the button that says 'click here'…
Bullshit – some managers use this term in a more general sense when

dealing with their staff, it means they want someone else to do the work.

Demographics
Meaning – the study of the characteristics of a consumer population or portion of, otherwise known as a **segment**.
Bullshit – with its pseudo-scientific overtones, this is perfect bullshit material; be seen to be an expert in the key demographics to your company and you'll be seen as a bit of a genius, the company bullshitter knows this and will want to give that impression too.

Differentiation
Meaning – many small companies can't compete with larger ones, especially on pricing, so they will concentrate on what makes them different. MDs will sometimes use it as a watch word, particularly if they operate in a market where they're up against stiff competition.
Bullshit – the marketing bullshitter uses this term when in meetings with the finance department as it gives the impression that they're being prudent. The term **point of difference** is used in the same context.

Door opener
Meaning – something in an advert or promotion that starts the **conversation** with the customer, that is after a **connection** with them has taken place.
Bullshit – once the door is open, you are mine…

Elasticity
Meaning – generally, it's applied to the relationship between the price of a product and its sales; the lower the price, the higher the sales, but when the price goes up, so sales go down, as though the relationship was elastic. Cigarettes are inelastic as no matter how much the price goes up, the poor addicted suckers keep buying them.
Bullshit – one of the great excuse words in marketing for the times when sales don't come through or their advert is a dog.

Feel good factor

Meaning – it's important that customers feel good about the products they buy and those companies that sell them, and executives will take care that any message or promotion signed off will have the right feel good factor.

Bullshit – it's an important part of the company bullshitter's strategy too, as the last thing they want is for their boss to have anything other than positive feelings toward them.

Going viral

Meaning – a state of nirvana for most advertisers is when their advert is so popular it gets sent from office to office and friend to friend via the Internet.

Bullshit – well bullshit is viral in many ways…

Hype

Meaning – inflated and over promotion, extra exposure, from the word Hypodermic.

Bullshit – hype is the lifeblood of every bullshitter.

Impacting

Meaning – promotions and advertising campaigns must have the right level of impact on those who they're aimed at and you'll hear managers often bang on about impacting displays and offers.

Bullshit – this isn't even a proper word, it's one purely designed to make the user look good.

Inspirational

Meaning – in this context, we want you to be so inspired by our products, we want you to spend your money on them…

Bullshit – telling you what we think you want to hear in the hope you'll spend some money on our products.

Keeper
Meaning – a keeper is a marketing technique used to encourage a customer to do something; it could be a prize or some sort of reward. See also *Door opener.*
Bullshit – usually classic bullshit and a form of legalised lying.

Market leading
Meaning – most companies dream of leading their chosen market; some dominant ones actually do, while some claim to actually widen or change the market with their latest products or campaigns. In reality, it's often got more to do with economic factors than marketing bullshit.
Bullshit – many companies kid themselves and their staff that they are market leading when in actual fact they are being complacent.

Market segments
Meaning – portions of a particular market based on age, wealth, regions, gender, etc...
Bullshit – the bullshitter will know their market segments, from ABC1s to Ds and Es, to Fit greys and Aspiring sophisticates, even Slobs. The cleverer sounding the term, the more likely the bullshitter is to use it as it makes them seem brighter. A colleague once attempted to impress the MD with his knowledge of market segments: 'which segment do I fit into?' he asked. The MD looked at his sheet and without thinking he said 'walking corpses'. He no longer works for that company.

Market share
Meaning – the proportion of a market achieved by a company.
Bullshit – bullshitters will use market share as a badge, but it's risky as it has **elasticity** and a price hike or a poor promotion could ruin it for them.

Mechanics and vehicles
Some would be forgiven in thinking that a conversation overheard in

a marketing department could be about cars, but a vehicle is the medium by which the promotional **message** is put across. While the term **mechanic** is actually the promotion itself, whether it is a three for two or a price cut.

Mega, Monster

Meaning – huge, extra, more.

Bullshit – no promotion or campaign simply does well, it has to be mega. Monster on the other hand is bigger than mega, it is extra huge!

Mind food

Meaning – books, newspapers and magazines are really mind food to nourish our brains.

Bullshit – if you believe that you believe anything…and your mind is probably dog food.

Must

Meaning – obligation, a requirement and inevitability.

Bullshit – an interesting change of meaning here as things become 'a must' or 'must have' item, a marketing manager's dream.

Niche

Meaning – niche marketing is in-vogue nowadays; websites and TV channels in particular go for ever smaller groups, hoping to tap into their interests and the high spending power devotees have.

Bullshit – niche groups are particularly open to exploitation as they spend more on their interests, but you need to be an expert to do it.

On message

Meaning – aware of what's going on, sticking to the company or party line.

Bullshit – a term made popular in the UK by Tony Blair and his spin doctors, woe betide any bullshitter that goes off message and isn't aware of what their boss wants.

Package
Meaning – the 'package' could be anything from a real box to a salary deal, but in this context, the executive will be looking for a collection of adverts, promotions and marketing which combined make the package.
Bullshit – the male bullshitter will talk about the size of the package as though it's something physical and you can be sure there's an inverse relationship working in there somewhere.

Paint a tapestry
Yes this has been witnessed; the user accompanied it with a sweeping wave of the hand and a winning smile. Tempted though we were to ask 'don't you mean picture?' we actually sat mute and thought 'Tosser'.

Paradigm
Meaning – taken from one of the major dictionaries: 'A set of assumptions, concepts, values and practices that constitutes a way of viewing reality for the community that shares them, especially in an intellectual discipline.' This book then is about the paradigm of bullshit. If it achieves a change in the behaviour of people and the way they use bullshit, then a **paradigm shift** would have taken place.
Bullshit – a word beloved of those who want to appear clever or well read in American business practices, they will talk about group and market paradigms without a clue what the word really means...but it *sounds* good.

Positioning
Meaning – sometimes in marketing known as **placement,** it's where your product or company is placed in relation to other products and companies in the market.
Bullshit – companies get very clever about product placement, for example, TV services being plugged in newspapers owned by the same company. For the competitive bullshitter, it is as always about them and how they are positioned in the corporate **bun fight** relation to their colleagues.

Proposition
Meaning – the offer.
Bullshit – marketing people like to use the term proposition because it has sexual overtones and they hope some of that will rub off on them.

Qualitative and quantitative research
Meaning – in qualitative research, you seek out people's attitudes and preferences, usually conducted through unstructured interviews or focus groups. For example, did Coca-Cola do enough qualitative research before they (disastrously for sales) changed the formula of Coke a few years back?
In quantitative research, you use measurement of consumer trends within a group. For example, one of the biggest crimes for manufacturers is to launch a product without doing the research on how many people are likely to want to buy it.
Bullshit – another piece of terminology which is great for sounding good but don't get them muddled up!

Sexy
Meaning – advertising campaigns can be described as sexy, not those featuring Claudia Schiffer, but those that do the job very successfully and create certain moist feelings about their products.
Bullshit – **sex it up** or **sexing it up** is the first thing any bullshitter thinks of in most situations, anything to make them look better.

Solutions
Meaning – open *Private Eye* and you'll find a weekly collection of 'solutions'; it's used to broaden the scope of a product or idea, so this book isn't a book to a retailer, it's a gift solution. An aspirin is a pain solution, a bed is a sleeping solution and a grave is a burial solution and so on. Whole departments and businesses have been created using this way of thinking…
Bullshit – an effective lying solution.

Target
Meaning – to aim something such as an advert at a specific market.
Bullshit – those doing their jobs will be targeting external consumers and markets, while the company bullshitter will target their internal opposition.

The customer is always right
Meaning – a slogan attributed to H. Gordon Selfridge, the founder of the Selfridge store in Oxford Street.
Bullshit – in reality it should say, 'the customer is always right, providing it doesn't cost too much money'.

Touchy feely, High touch – low tech
Meaning – close physically, emotional, open to feelings, easy to understand.
Bullshit – artistic, marketing and advertising people are renowned for their touchy feely approach to work; this leaves the rest of the business distinctly uncomfortable and suspicious as they would, in general, like to leave their emotions hidden thanks very much.

USP
Meaning – the **Unique Selling Point** for any company is essential to **differentiate** themselves from their competitors.
Bullshit – the company bullshitter will also have a USP to make them stand out; they will be known for something positive that will help their careers and keep them ahead of the competition.

Value added
Meaning – something of value given or included.
Bullshit – the trick is to appear to give a lot but not give much…

Water cooler campaign
Meaning – something that is so exciting it's discussed in the office the next day, as everyone congregates around water coolers.
Bullshit – when have you ever seen people hanging round water

coolers? It doesn't happen! OK maybe the odd sad perv, in the hope someone young might appear.

Wavelength
Meaning – in harmony, several departments working well together on the same thing, see also **on message**.
Bullshit – would a bullshitter be on the same wavelength as us when reading this book? Probably not, they'd use it as a personal bullshit manual...

Winning hearts and minds
Meaning – persuading, bringing people on to your side by doing good.
Bullshit – another term made popular by New Labour, they did it before the election, they did it before the war and to the Iraqis after the war and there's a bullshitter doing it to you.

Wordsmith
Meaning – a fluent writer, to edit a text to improve it.
Bullshit – the top bullshitter will never let something (especially with their name on) go before a superior or the public without signing it off and ensuring it says exactly what it should. They don't edit though, they wordsmith.

Wow factor
Meaning – something in a campaign, product or idea that makes you go wow!
Bullshit – advertisers and their clients will always be looking to add that certain something to whatever they are selling; some call it an extra layer of bullshit.

The brand
Brand image is incredibly important to any company and this image that their brand projects can make or break them. For example, Gerald Ratner's famous speech in which he stated that what he sold

was 'crap' destroyed the dream for many who had bought jewellery in his stores.

The brand is often well used by company leaders as an effective way to give their employees a sense of focus and belonging, as for Ratner, his business suffered accordingly after his speech and it is seen as one of the biggest business errors and a lesson to us all. In other words, you need at least a little bullshit to survive; it doesn't pay to be too honest.

Here are some terms to watch out for...

Badge item
Meaning – a piece of clothing or product that says something about your lifestyle and values.
Bullshit – advertisers kill to get this level of acceptance for their products; meanwhile the company bullshitter will be picking the right badge items to make them look good around the office.

Brandalism, Brandroid
You know who they are – Formula 1 cars, Supermarket Own Label ranges, Burger Chains and many more, all guilty of overusing their brands, putting them everywhere on their products and in their advertising, the cheeky monkeys.

A **Brandroid** is someone who has bought the company line completely, who then automatically spouts company slogans and lives their life according to the values of the company. Usually a sad individual who should know better, and in their heart of hearts, they probably do.

Brandwidth
Meaning – the level of recognition awarded to a product within a market.
Bullshit – the level of recognition awarded to the bullshitter within

their office. Probably should be called bullwidth.

Iconic

Meaning – an iconic brand is Coca-Cola who has heritage, huge sales and popularity, plus a global reach.

Bullshit – many companies kid themselves that their brand fits into this category and many a strategy has gone awry because they have underestimated the general apathy of the general public. Celebrities have a similar issue; many act like they are A-list **icons** when they're definitely not. The amazing thing is that we let them get away with it.

Off brand

Meaning – not advertised with the correct values, or unsympathetic to the brand.

Bullshit – as with off-message it's a desperate situation when your advertising company advertises your product as something it's not and with values you don't subscribe too. Bullshitters beware.

BULLSHIT BINGO – *Marketing*

PARADIGM	MARKET SEGMENT	BRAND IMAGE	USP	WOW FACTOR	INSPIRATIONAL	IMPACTFUL	VALUE
ICONIC	MEGA	ENERGY	DEMOGRAPHICS	CONNECT	WAVELENGTH	GAME PLAN	MUST
CONSUMER AGENDA	EDUCATING CUSTOMERS	SOLUTION	ON MESSAGE	BRAINSTORM	HYPE	THE BRAND	ALIGN
BLUE SKY	VIRAL	RAMP IT UP	HOLISTIC	MECHANIC	EMPOWER	FOCUS	WINNING HEARTS AND MINDS
VEHICLE	TARGET	CUSTOMER	LOYALTY	INSPIRE	HALO EFFECT	HEAVYWEIGHT	POINT OF DIFFERENCE
PACKAGE	NICHE	FEEL GOOD FACTOR	EMPATHY	CALL TO ACTION	RATCHET	MONSTER	TOUCHY FEELY

How to play: simply tick off six words in one meeting and shout out BINGO!

Conference bullshit

Conferences are essentially all about bullshit, where the MD will tell you how the company is doing, choosing each word carefully, politically, often being completely over the top and behaving in an unnaturally jaunty way.

It's a time when heads of departments give their presentations, when the management come over all motivational and there's very little real honesty.

PowerPoint is the bullshitter's tool of choice as it can be used to hide all sorts of problems. Watch out for people whose graphs and figures can't be read, or who have more than five bullet points to a slide and more pictures than words, they're probably bullshitting about something.

The words and phrases used in conferences are spread around this book but there's one area of bullshit unique to them and that's the music that's used to heighten the atmosphere and create the right mood.

Here's our top ten conference tunes, designed to set the mood and rally the troops.

1. Simply The Best – Tina Turner
2. We Are The Champions – Queen
3. Ready To Go – Republica
4. Chariots Of Fire – Vangelis
5. Show Me The Hero – M People
6. All Together Now – The Farm
7. Let Me Entertain You – Robbie Williams
8. Fanfare For The Common Man – Aaron Copeland
9. Sunshine On A Rainy Day – Zoe
10. Money – Pink Floyd

See the conference music bingo card; let us know your conference heroes.

BULLSHIT BINGO – Conference music

FANFARE FOR THE COMMON MAN COPELAND	THE JAMES BOND THEME TUNE	READY TO GO REPUBLICA	BOYS ARE BACK IN TOWN THIN LIZZIE	LET ME ENTERTAIN YOU ROBBIE WILLIAMS	WITH A LITTLE HELP FROM MY FRIENDS BEATLES	THRILLER MICHAEL JACKSON	CHARIOTS OF FIRE VANGELIS	MONEY FOR NOTHING DIRE STRAITS	WHILE YOU SEE A CHANCE STEVE WINWOOD
CARS GARY NUMAN	JUMP VAN HALEN	EVERYBODY WANTS TO RULE THE WORLD TEARS FOR FEARS	IN THE AIR TONIGHT PHIL COLLINS	ALL TOGETHER NOW THE FARM	LOVE IS ALL AROUND WET WET WET	MONEY'S TOO TIGHT TO MENTION SIMPLY RED	BORN TO RUN BRUCE SPRINGSTEEN	SIMPLY THE BEST TINA TURNER	EVERY LITTLE THING SHE DOES IS MAGIC POLICE
ONE MORE TIME DAFTPUNK	BEAUTIFUL DAY U2	JUMPIN' JACK FLASH ROLLING STONES	WE ARE THE CHAMPIONS QUEEN	WHAT A WONDERFUL WORLD LOUIS ARMSTRONG	SMOKE ON THE WATER DEEP PURPLE	REBEL REBEL DAVID BOWIE	THANK YOU DIDO	TWO TRIBES FRANKIE GOES TO HOLLYWOOD	THE WORLD IS NOT ENOUGH GARBAGE
MY HEART WILL GO ON CELINE DION	SEARCH FOR THE HERO M PEOPLE	EYE OF THE TIGER SURVIVOR	SUNSHINE ON A RAINY DAY ZOE	MONEY PINK FLOYD	RUN SNOW PATROL	ALL YOU NEED IS LOVE BEATLES	IT'S A KIND OF MAGIC QUEEN	GOOD THING FINE YOUNG CANNIBALS	I BELIEVE I CAN FLY R KELLY

How to play: simply tick off four songs in one conference and shout out BINGO!

9. Human Resources and people

"I wish all the people who have trouble communicating would just shut up."

Tom Lehrer

Human Resources and people
Sometimes known as the people team, the HR department manage recruitment and handle dismissals and layoffs plus a whole host of issues in between. You have to feel sympathy for them as they must receive more bullshit than most, but as you'll see, they're often the best at giving it too.

The **Peter Principle** states that employees within an organisation will advance to their highest level of competence and then be promoted to and remain at a level at which they are incompetent. It is amazing how true this is and how those who were fantastic as a worker are often basically incompetent as a manager.

The common denominator is people; once the worker becomes a manager, the whole dynamic changes and bullshit comes into play.

HR vocabulary
There's a language used here to soften blows, to take out confrontation and prepare people for the worst...otherwise known as HRPR.

Here are some terms you may be familiar with...

Assessment, Appraisal, Review
Meaning – workers are scored on a set of criteria to determine their progress, set objectives and their training needs.
Bullshit – the lifeblood of HR, the time when all the bullshitting and planning come together, the time to shine, the time to get easy objectives for the next review.

Career planning
Meaning – planning the long-term career, with personal needs in mind as well as the company's.
Bullshit – on joining a company, the bullshitter will know largely what jobs they'll want to aim for and plan accordingly. Those naïve enough to believe their managers have their careers at heart will be sorely treated; the number one rule in career planning is look after number one.

Check in/Check out
Meaning – in some companies, the caring world of HR is a little extreme; before any meeting happens people are asked to check-in their feelings at the beginning and check-out their feelings at the end.
Bullshit – thinking 'oh for God's sake, just get on with it!' Saying 'I feel really privileged to work for this company…'

Coaching
Meaning – a recent trend is to have a coach, usually an experienced ex-business person who will help company managers to become better at their jobs.
Bullshit – bullshitting seems to require no coaching…

Collegiate
Meaning – able to work well with others.
Bullshit – appearing to be able to work well with others.

Core competences
Meaning – the things you know how to do, the things you're good at.

Bullshit – with seemingly supernatural abilities, the company bullshitter will seem to know exactly which areas it's worth being good at and what not to bother with.

Cream always rises to the top
Meaning – the best people always rise to the top echelons of the business.
Bullshit – shit floats too…

Dedicated Resource
Meaning – a person or team working on a specific project or role.
Bullshit – a good way of justifying the expansion of a team, dedicated resource is needed for each specific task; the idea is to get a bigger team with higher costs, so that a pay rise request is justified for the extra responsibility.

Dotted line
Meaning – part of the reporting structure in a large organisation where someone, while not being the boss, has control over another's work, hence a dotted line responsibility.
Bullshit – great for the company bullshitter, because it enables them to play them off with the real boss, to the bullshitter's benefit of course.

Downtime
Meaning – a period of time when something, either a system or factory, isn't operating i.e. when tools are downed.
Bullshit – this probably isn't a good thing but always a good opportunity to improve scores at Minesweeper.

Drinking at the last chance saloon
Meaning – always on the verge of being sacked, or when applied more broadly, going bust.
Bullshit – usually a victim of someone else's bullshit.

A fish rots from the head down
Meaning – basically a reference to the performance of the head of a company, the implication being that if they leave the company will flounder (geddit?).
Bullshit – it works another way, as a company head's influence on a company is so great that if they are poor, then the whole business will suffer.

Golden handcuffs, handshake, hello, parachute
Meaning – a good thing whatever the situation as it means a payment of some description and an incentive to stay or go.
Bullshit – the company bullshitters will position themselves at the front of the queue whatever happens…

Knowledge worker
Meaning – people who actually know what they are doing and have some skills.
Bullshit – people whose chameleon-like skills enable them to look like they know what they're doing…

Learning curve
Meaning – a graphic depiction of the rate of learning, of progress in learning, a skill against the time required to master it.
Bullshit – at the start, this imaginary curve is very steep, as experience is gained it flattens out to a shallow incline; it doesn't seem to register apathy though.

Mentoring
Meaning – the process of senior managers guiding the junior executives with their career.
Bullshit – it has the potential to be a bit like thieves turning out to be better thieves after serving time in prison.

Mindset

Meaning – often used to refer to someone who isn't doing a good job; '*their heart's not in it*' or their '*head's not in the right place*'. Whatever, apparently it's all down to mindset and their mental attitude.
Bullshit – projecting the right mindset is key whatever the situation.

Objective

Meaning – target, outcome.
Bullshit – usually given as part of the **appraisal** procedure, the trick is to get easy objectives while the person setting them thinks they're hard.

One team

Meaning – the motivational side of HR will always try to break down barriers between departments and teams, mainly using the 'we're all one team' mantra.
Bullshit – it doesn't work of course but everyone pretends it does.

Open door policy

Meaning – the HR department want to give the impression that they are always accessible and available to solve problems.
Bullshit – an opportunity to get the gossip and spread it.

Partnership

Meaning – HR departments always work in partnership with their colleagues.
Bullshit – company bullshitters look like they work in partnership but are out for themselves.

Personal growth

Meaning – getting more mature, acquiring knowledge and skills.
Bullshit – despite appearances and what is told, this is actually a personal responsibility; don't expect too much company support.

Skill set
Meaning – the skills you have.
Bullshit – the skills I want to give the impression I have.

Square peg in a round hole
Meaning – a person whose skills and job role don't match.
Bullshit – usually most of the senior management in any company.

Structure
Meaning – every business has a structure and a hierarchy and it's usually the job of the HR team to administer it. There are **flat structures** where hierarchy is minimised and optimal **restructures** geared to efficiency.
Bullshit – the weak personalities will end up with smaller jobs and smaller teams, the **big guns** will get bigger teams and bigger offices, the clever company bullshitter will work within this giving the impression their needs are paramount.

Succession planning
Meaning – plans are made so that when one person leaves a job, another is ready to step in.
Bullshit – the reality is that it never really happens as opinions on people change daily and either staff turnover is too high or too low to make it work effectively.

Team building
Meaning – many managers really care about how their teams work with each other; it's a real science to some. Often this aspect is delegated to the HR folk who will organise **away days** where the team works on a series of exercises designed to get them working together in harmony.
Bullshit – yeah right…

Virtual team, virtual manager
Meaning – a group of people who work on one thing, the difference being that they don't go to a physical office, they work remotely and are managed remotely too.
Bullshit – a good place for a skive.

Getting the sack – the bullshit terms
We all know instances where companies have informed their staff of their loss of employment by the media, even via text message, and here are some of the most common terms. Essentially they all add up to the same thing…you're out!

Axed, bust, chop, cut, fire, terminate – indicates a forced removal or at least on the grounds of some sort of misconduct.

Canning, canned, ditch, sack – indicates that the person being **shown the door** is something to be ashamed of, the company concerned doesn't want to **wash their dirty washing in public**.

Collect your P45 – for those of you not in the UK, the P45 is a personal document that passes between employers, it's given to the employee as they leave.

Constructive dismissal, forced resignation – some managers have this down to a fine art, making their employees' lives hell so that they leave 'voluntarily', saving the manager from paying them off. It's difficult to prove and fraught with bullshit.

De-recruit, downsize, re-engineer, restructure, right-size – all terms used to make the fact that a company is sacking lots of people more palatable and to give the impression that more is being done aside from just sacking.

Dismissed, get the boot, marching orders – more militaristic over-tones and the impression that there is a lack of honour in the going of the person being sacked.

Drinking at the last chance saloon – this usually prior to the event and unbeknown to the person being sacked.

I want him/her out – the cry of a manager desperate to get rid of someone, usually to the HR team who then have to facilitate the exit, usually by transferring occasionally by more devious means – 'go now with a good reference or later with a bad one.'

Lay off, let go – an attempt to soften the blow by softening the words – it doesn't work.

Redundancy – the process by which companies reduce their staff. For some, this carries the wrong overtones who prefer it all to be voluntary or to have it said that they resign.

Resign – to jack in your job and go to work for someone else can be very satisfying, until you realise you're just listening to the same old bullshit.

Recruitment bullshit

Open the Sunday papers at the jobs pages and bullshit abounds, from describing Swindon as 'nestled between the Marlborough Downs and the rolling Cotswold Hills' to the kidology of 'you'll be leading a team'. Here are some of the job advert favourites and what they really mean...

Achievement oriented – thank god because we don't give a shit.
Clarity of vision – because we haven't a clue what to do next.
Commercial acumen – we need someone who knows what a P&L is.
Communication skills – no one is talking to each other and we need you to mediate.

Decision maker – we need someone to blame.

Development – get them before they develop enough skills to be classed as a senior manager, they're cheaper.

Dynamic – well someone needs to do the work.

Energetic – now you've finished that, the boss's car needs washing.

Enthusiastic – we need someone who likes our ideas.

Exciting – because we aren't, we're boring.

Flair – because we don't want another boring git.

Highly organised – thank god, because we're in a mess...

Innovative – we don't want boring people in our company. Also read as young.

Interpersonal skills – someone who can actually talk to other people without embarrassment or being embarrassing.

Leading – well we are; in Berkshire.

Lifestyle – no working class people need apply.

Make a difference – because we've run out of ideas.

Money motivated – low salary, high bonus and unachievable targets.

Negotiation skills – all our deals are just rubbish.

Numerate – we need someone who knows how to work Excel.

Opportunities – risks, or at least the chance to clear up someone else's mess.

Portfolio – we want you to do other things too, but we haven't thought what they could be and we thought this might make the job sound bigger than it really is.

Presentation skills – because we're scared of PowerPoint.

Proven success – success would be nice, maybe it will rub off on to us too.

Reputation – great you've done it before.

Stakeholder – if we like you we'll give you some shares, eventually.

Step up to the challenge – because we can't.

Supportive – we need a brown noser, to tell us how great we are.

Team building skills – we can't manage them, we need you...

The bullshitter's guide to office characters

Remember the aim of the company bullshitter is to make themselves look as good as possible, in order to get promoted, get a salary rise or just to be seen by their boss in the best light. Here are the bullshitter's victims and competitors, not forgetting those who inspire and those to suck up to.

Adequate, Inarticulate
Someone who is expert at their job, but can't explain why or what actions should be taken without getting tongue tied and frustrated.
Motto – *I can't explain why but it will work.*

Articulate inadequate
A common sight in offices around the world, the Articulate inadequate looks great and sounds great but in practice hasn't a clue.
Motto – *looking good* (usually while looking in the mirror).

Deceptionist
A good deceptionist is worth their weight in gold to a company; a deceptionist will make everyone's life hell, requiring rewards almost every time they're asked to do something, however menial.
Motto – *over my dead body.*

Hyperactive
Referred to as **hyper,** this person will rush around the office in a near panic while not actually achieving or doing any real work.
Motto – *it's a nightmare, oh my God!*

Influencer
This is the most subtle of individuals, having good **influencing skills** is essential to the bullshitter, it gets things done and gets you noticed.
Motto – *maybe I shouldn't say this but…*

Jobsworth
A widely hated figure, the jobsworth will do exactly what is required, or what they are contracted to do, no more and no less. They deserve all the abuse the bullshitter can muster.
Motto – *it's not my job…*

Journeyman

The journeyman will go from job to job, company to company, without really achieving anything much. They're happy being average, keeping their heads down and earning money in a quiet but generally efficient way.

Motto – *keep your head down.*

Lame duck

There's always a weakling someone who is picked on, someone who is a permanent victim and someone who the bullshitter uses as a stooge. A lame duck manager is one who is covering a role for a while or who is on the way out.

Motto – *um, no thanks, ok yes, right...*

Manager of the manager

Their primary skill is **managing upwards**, keeping their manager sweet and making them think all their decisions are their own; the managing manager is one of the most subtle and successful of all bullshitters.

Motto – *it's up to you Guv, you're the boss after all...*

Misery

A person so long in the tooth and so unhappy in their work and their life, they cause disruption in any office; often they haven't the where-withal to leave or feel if they hang on a little longer they may get a pay off.

Motto – *nothing works.*

Motivator

This is the person (mainly men it has to be said) who gets up in front of the team on a wet Friday morning in January and shouts 'Woah! Goood Moooorrrning!' and then to the muted response, he says, 'What was that? I can't hear you!' while cupping a hand to the ear. His job is to 'motivate the troops' and is generally quite useful to have around but mostly is just bloody irritating. Motivators are usually unconsciously the biggest users of business bullshit, though they are not usually bullshitters.

Motto – *are you feeling good?* (said very loudly).

Movers and shakers

The bullshitter's nightmare, people who actually do something, who make things happen. It is said that in a company of 1000 people, the real work is done by about 20 people. They can be very senior or very junior but they work like Trojans.

Motto – *J.F.D.I. (Just Fucking Do it…)* or *Leading from the front.*

Nerd

A useful bit part player in any bullshitter's life, the nerd knows technical things that they can use to find out information or make their lives easier. The nerd is not necessarily a techie but just an expert or real specialist; they're all the same to the bullshitter. The nerds themselves live in their own world, untouched by the machinations of business; the people that are referred to by them are 'users'.

Motto – *I know therefore I am.*

Organiser

Someone who plans and organises the office parties, charity collections, events and anything else that means they don't have to do their actual jobs.

Motto – *let me do that…*

Players

To the bullshitter, nearly everyone is a player, a competitor, someone to get or be aware of and someone to be used or stepped on for career gain.

Motto – *winning is everything.*

Political animals

The bullshitter is the archetypal political animal using spin, lies, deceit and pushing the image of overwhelming honesty to get to where they want to be.

Motto – *to succeed in politics, it is often necessary to rise above your principles.*

Scapegoat

Any bullshitter worth their salt will have a scapegoat lined up, whatever the situation.

Self Toaster

Many offices have someone who always says what they think, too honest to be aware of the consequences of their words, too decent to tell lies when it's needed. They are happy to score personal **own goals** if they think the situation demands it. The boss will tolerate it to a point but eventually they will go too far and they'll be sacked. This process is called self toasting. The bullshitter will prime the self toaster to their advantage, for their own ends of course.

Motto – *I'm right (that's the important thing)* or *Naming and shaming.*

Snake in the grass

A key skill of the bullshitter is to rat on their colleagues and friends. The snake will do it as a matter of course and their manager will love them for it.

Motto – *oh, what a tangled web we weave, when first we practise to deceive…*

Stakeholders

A stakeholder puts their neck on the line for a business or project; the stake may be financial or a reputation, but whichever, it's fodder for the bullshitter to exploit.

Motto – *show me the money!*

Status seekers

Those whose whole aim is to get to the next level in the management structure to improve their standing in the company. The bullshitter will take advantage of them as, being status seekers themselves, they will know what it takes to get under their skin.

Motto – *profit without honour.*

Team player

Like the journeyman, the team player will be happy playing their role in the team with no leadership ambitions. The bullshitter will exploit the best of them in their team to make themselves look good in the process.

Motto – *for the team!*

Wearer of dead men's shoes

A manager so long in the job who does just enough to keep it and hold up the bullshitter's career progression, they are often well practised in the art of bullshit and for this reason, the ambitious bullshitter's worst enemy.

Motto – *thou shall not pass*!

See also our section on management types on page 17.

BULLSHIT BINGO – *Human Resources*

PARTNERSHIP	REDUNDANT	SUCCESSION PLANNING	MINDSET	HARMONY	APPRAISAL	RECRUIT-MENT POLICY	TEAM BUILDING	EXCITED
ONE TEAM	TEAM	SKILL SET	CAREER PLAN	HUDDLE	TOGETHER	VISION	CLARITY	ENERGY
PORTFOLIO	ACUMEN	CHALLENGE	ATTITUDE	INTER-PERSONAL SKILLS	REPUTATION	GETS THINGS DONE	MOTIVATOR	NUMERATE
INNOVATIVE	ACHIEVE-MENT	LIFESTYLE	ASSESSMENT	TEAM PLAYER	ABILITY	MENTOR	DYNAMIC	OPEN DOOR
AWARE	COACH	CORE COMPETENCE	STAKE-HOLDER	CUT	CHECK IN	DOTTED LINE	OPPOR-TUNITY	ORGANISER

How to play: simply tick off five words in one meeting and shout out BINGO!

BULLSHIT BINGO – Managers giving career advice

CARVE OUT A NICHE	CONVERT PLANS INTO ACTION	HIDDEN AGENDA	RESULTS DRIVEN	YOU CAN DO IT IF YOU BELIEVE YOU CAN	YOU SCRATCH MY BACK AND I'LL SCRATCH YOURS	IT WILL BE THE MAKING OF YOU	GRAVITAS
WILL TO WIN	COMFORT ZONE	NO PRESSURE	TENACIOUS	HUNGRY	IT'S A JUNGLE OUT THERE	SINK OR SWIM	EYES AND EARS
HIT THE GROUND RUNNING	PROFILE	KNOWLEDGE	NO IS NOT IN MY VOCABULARY	FAST TRACK	INCENTIVES	FINAL PIECE OF THE JIGSAW	DON'T ROCK THE BOAT
PROACTIVE	GRASP THE NETTLE	PRODUCE THE GOODS	GO THE EXTRA MILE	WORK ETHIC	LEARNING	PRIORITIZE	TIME MANAGE-MENT
EYE ON THE PRIZE	FOOD CHAIN	QUID PRO QUO	WORK SMARTER	PROACTION NOT REACTION	SURVIVAL OF THE FITTEST	KNOW-HOW	LEAN AND MEAN
LONG HAUL	MANAGING EXPECTATIONS	ALIGNMENT	FREE RIDE	BANG THE DRUM	LEVELS OF HONESTY	ON THE MAP	OUTCOME

How to play: simply tick off five words in one meeting and shout out BINGO!

10. Planes, boats, cars and trains

"Going to work for a large company is like getting on a train. Are you going sixty miles an hour or is the train going sixty miles an hour and you're just sitting still?"

J Paul Getty

Planes, boats, cars and trains...
Much management bullshit is derived from various modes of transport, which is a little weird but people seem to love using the analogies; it is catching, just try it when next in a meeting. Mention something like 'we could be cycling with no saddle here' and watch as the other attendees start wheeling out their favourite transport metaphors; there you see, even I'm doing it now.

Bumpy ride
Meaning – a difficult time.
Bullshit – usually caused by someone undermining the work in question.

Cycling with no saddle
Meaning – very uncomfortable.
Bullshit – not really bullshit but everyone winces.

Deep diving
Meaning – detailed examination, in depth analysis.
Bullshit – brainstorming but supposedly with more thought and insight.

Drive
Meaning – push, make sure things happen, passion, ambition.
Bullshit – people with drive are generally treated with some suspicion by colleagues as they tend to be slightly scary.

Fast lane, fast track
Meaning – in the fast lane means going faster than everyone else, more exciting.
Bullshit – that's what they'd like you to believe any way.

Fine tuning
Meaning – the finishing touches to a piece of work.
Bullshit – the final bit of added bullshit.

Flight path, flight plan
Meaning – the route to take, how something such as a project is progressing, also used is on track, or tracking
Bullshit – also referred to by some as the **journey**, some just love this, talking about **navigational aids, turbulence, mid-air refuelling, runway lights** and **landings**, makes you want to throw up. **It will never fly** is the negative version.

Fly, Flying
Meaning – to go fast.
Bullshit – one for sales people, they're always flying or at least that's what they'd like everyone to think.

Flying by the seat of your pants
Meaning – working using personal judgement and gut feel rather than to a predetermined plan.
Bullshit – companies like to give the impression that they are free thinking and encourage risk takers; in reality, few will give too many personal freedoms.

Free ride
Meaning – getting a benefit for no cost.
Bullshit – for the bullshitter, there's always someone who will pay.

Get out of first gear
Meaning – accelerating, improving the speed at which something is done.
Bullshit – used when something is stuck or not being done very fast. If a bullshitter is involved, then there's a good reason why it's in the doldrums; either they want to show someone up or they want to get fired.

Going on autopilot
Meaning – doing something without conscious thought.
Bullshit – applies to most jobs that involve long hours at a computer, although this could be described as going on to screensaver.

Green light
Meaning – go ahead.
Bullshit – apparently some managers actually like to say 'give it the green light' or 'green light it' – how naff is that?

Keep the engine running
Meaning – to keep something on hold with the expectation that when it does start, it needs to be up and running quickly.
Bullshit – alternatively keep something on hold until someone pays up, then get out of there as fast as you can...

Land
Meaning – to finish something.
Bullshit – a classic but see **flight path** for more aviation shenanigans.

Park it
Meaning – put it to one side until later.

Bullshit – the real meaning is 'put it to one side and don't mention it again'.

Radar
Meaning – to take notice, to get noticed.
Bullshit – are you on the boss's radar? The bullshitter will be…

Reinvent the wheel
Meaning – to create something that already exists.
Bullshit – as someone once said 'there are no new ideas, just old ones rehashed' or something like that…

Road map
Meaning – a bit like a flight path but less straightforward.
Bullshit – another one to revel in, with **pit stops, barriers, detours, lay-bys** and the odd **breakdown**.

Rocket science
Meaning – something incredibly complicated, usually used in the negative, 'it's not rocket science, after all' when referring to something simple that has been done poorly.
Bullshit – well except rocket science itself, nothing actually is rocket science is it?

Steer
Meaning – influence.
Bullshit – a good bullshit word if ever there was one…

Tailspin
Meaning – uncontrolled descent.
Bullshit – if this is being used then something has gone drastically wrong, time to enjoy the discomfort of others or just get the coat.

Up to speed
Meaning – fully informed.
Bullshit – the top bullshitter is always up to speed.

11. Sporting bullshit and clichés

"Business is a good game – lots of competition and a minimum of rules. You keep score with money."

Nolan Bushnell

Sporting bullshit and clichés
Many managers borrow their sayings from sports, although the sport itself offers up many clichés too. Several sports have their own specific language and contributions, some of which have found their way into our lives; these are included also.

Football seems to provide more clichés and silly phrases than any sport and as a tribute to that, we've included a card especially for viewers of *Match of the Day*; with this, you can sit down with your beer and crisps and mark off the terms as Hansen, Lineker and friends come out with them; it should take all of five minutes.

Ambassador (for the game)
Meaning – a representative with authority.
Bullshit – usually a player with some pedigree and a fair degree of gravitas, companies like to develop people who can play an ambassadorial role, usually dealing with trade organisations rather than doing any actual work.

Ball park
Meaning – in the region of.
Bullshit – an imprecise term but one that most companies work to even it they like to think they are being accurate in their predictions.

Big match temperament
Meaning – the ability to shine when under pressure or in the spotlight.
Bullshit – so your presentation was excellent and you defended your bad results with aplomb, you will go far…

Bread and butter
Meaning – the usual, everyday means of support or income.
Bullshit – companies who take their bread and butter revenue for granted are the ones to avoid, complacency rules…

Bung
Meaning – a bribe, a discrete reward.
Bullshit – now synonymous particularly with football transfers, bung is also pretty common in the corporate world, they're just better at disguising it.

Bystander, in the audience, in the crowd
Meaning – to stand by and watch the action.
Bullshit – are you in the stands watching the game or are you on the pitch as a player…oh please!

Class, class act
Meaning – stylish, elegant, achievement with aplomb.
Bullshit – managers want class acts in their teams, whether it's a corporation or a sport; it's the interpretation of what 'class' means that is the problem.

Come of age
Meaning – to grow up, mature and gain independence. Young players mature from youth to experience, usually in a particularly tough match where they heavily feature showing their skills for the first time; some maintain form, while most turn into **old lags** or **journeymen** or disappear, never to be seen again.
Bullshit – in corporate culture, this is usually applied to someone who

though young and previously anonymous, suddenly does a good piece of work or an excellent presentation. To the company bullshitter, they are a **clear and present danger** and must be dealt with.

Counter punch
Meaning – from boxing, an attack, straight after your opponent has attacked.
Bullshit – the top company bullshitter will always have something ready to get back at a competing bullshitter.

Cover all bases
Meaning – from baseball, to take everything into account.
Bullshit – the province of the conscientious company bullshitter, they won't miss a trick.

Curve ball
Meaning – from baseball, a tricky and unexpected problem.
Bullshit – plenty of these in business without the help of your friendly neighbourhood bullshit merchant. An English, cricketing equivalent may be **bowled a bouncer.**

Done fantastic
Meaning – from football, performed well. English footballers and managers always leave off the 'ly' in any word that needs it and substitute 'done' for 'did', for example, **the boy done fantastic.**
Bullshit – some managers talk in this way in an effort to get some street cred, but somehow it wouldn't sound quite as good if it came out as 'the boy performed fantastically'.

Dream team
Meaning – the best combination of team members.
Bullshit – times are good, profits are high, there are no personnel issues, everyone in the team is performing very well, therefore it follows it's a great team, a dream team. This is the time to start making changes before it all goes tits up.

Early doors
Meaning – from football, early in the game.
Bullshit – its origins are to do with the early opening of the doors in pubs, another one of those phrases that the more earnest managers use to make them sound like they're really one of the lads.

Even keel
Meaning – from yachting, keeping things steady and trouble free.
Bullshit – at some stage in their career, every manager discovers that, like golf, sailing is the thing to get into if you want promotion.

Final score
Meaning – the result.
Bullshit – imagine the MD, having set the over ambitious budgets and targets, turning to the harassed finance team and saying 'So what's the final score?' Of course they know the figures are rubbish but self preservation will win over and they will give a favourable answer in the hope they can find something extra to **fill the gap** during the year ahead.

Fire, Full on, Passion, Pace, Pride, Total commitment
Meaning – passion, urgency, aggression, will to win.
Bullshit – many play their sport with fire in the belly, a few managers use it as a management technique and when they do, most people just take the piss.

From left field
Meaning – from baseball, something outside the norm, unexpected.
Bullshit – not a popular event with bullshitters, who like to be in control.

Game of two halves
Meaning – from football, a post-match review classic. A good example is the 2005 European Cup Final where Liverpool went three goals behind after an awful first half performance; in the second half, they

levelled the match, playing like a different team.
Bullshit – a term often nabbed by financial managers in presentations to the city, in a matey attempt to explain the variable financial performance of their company, of course the financial journalists see straight through it and immediately sense that something is wrong.

Game plan
Meaning – from American sports, the planned tactics for playing the game.
Bullshit – everyone has one of these, one for doing your work and one for dealing with your colleagues.

Goal
Meaning – from football, the target.
Bullshit – goals are the lifeblood for ambitious managers everywhere, the company bullshitter will have goals too, aside from the publicly known.

Go for it
Meaning – do it, with gusto.
Bullshit – most managers who 'go for it' see themselves as great leaders; most managers who encourage others with the term are usually great avoiders.

Good engine
Meaning – lots of stamina.
Bullshit – prepared to work late (probably with no pay).

Head held high
Meaning – proud, with dignity.
Bullshit – usually the thing to do when it all goes wrong.

Heavyweight
Meaning – from boxing, important, with gravitas.
Bullshit – or just fat.

Hit the ground running
Meaning – start something as if already experienced, after lots of preparation.
Bullshit – an impression you must give.

Hungry
Meaning – eager, keen, ambitious.
Bullshit – even if they don't feel it, the bullshit merchant will always act it.

In two minds
Meaning – uncertain (what to do next).
Bullshit – should have been a goal there, should have made that sale…

In with the big boys now
Meaning – playing with top clubs or players, top companies, experienced and senior executives.
Bullshit – the implication being that they are much more important, mainly because of the direct relationship between money and importance, like nothing else matters.

It's a funny game
Meaning – anything unusual can happen.
Bullshit – yes so?

Level playing field
Meaning – everything being equal.
Bullshit – one of the great excuses, 'it's not a level playing field boss, I can't include that in my budget, it's not fair…'

Lightweight
Meaning – from boxing, unimportant, no gravitas.
Bullshit – male managers often say this about female managers.

Move the goal posts
Meaning – to change the parameters and adjust targets.
Bullshit – if it doesn't look like they are going to hit their targets, the bullshitters will change the rules or the parameters to their favour. Make sure you know who the bullshitters are; if they approach you with a proposal in the run up to **year end**, make yourself scarce.

Next level
Meaning – to improve performance from one perceived level to the next.
Bullshit – if you can get to the next level, we'll give you a bonus, pay rise, better car, improved pension…yeah right.

On a sticky wicket
Meaning – from cricket, a dodgy position.
Bullshit – that's where most managers are, for most of the time.

Plain sailing
Meaning – from sailing, to finish with no complications.
Bullshit – remember that other cliché about the swan looking serene on the surface while paddling furiously under the surface, same thing.

Played out of our skins, played with their hearts out
Meaning – play so hard, bits of body fall off or get exposed.
Bullshit – not a pretty sight.

Play hardball
Meaning – from baseball, play it tough.
Bullshit – an impression some managers want to give rather than the reality; most are sneakier…

Pump iron
Meaning – from bodybuilding, it's the high associated with heavy-weight training.

Bullshit – used to say we're building up for a fight or building up the company in some way.

Punch above his/her weight
Meaning – from boxing, do better than expected or than their abilities would suggest.
Bullshit – very scary for the bullshitter who wants control and predictability.

Put some skin in the game
Meaning – a euphemism for making an investment.
Bullshit – sounds faintly disgusting, therefore good bullshit, possibly to do with leather balls, but can you imagine anyone with an English accent really saying this…

Sea change
Meaning – from sailing, a major change in the weather or state of the sea.
Bullshit – initiating a sea change is a rare event, usually big changes happen by chance or when actions are delayed until it's too late.

Step up to the plate
Meaning – from baseball, be counted, take up the challenge.
Bullshit – only for the naïve or ambitious.

Sucker punch
Meaning – from boxing, an unexpected successful attack.
Bullshit – something the bullshit expert lives for.

Take one game at a time
Meaning – from football, advice not to overstretch but just concentrate on the immediate future and all will be OK.
Bullshit – or push your head in the sand and hope the problems go away.

Up and under
Meaning – from rugby, term for a hopeful high ball popularised by the late Eddy Wareing.
Bullshit – a situation where something good will happen, you can watch the bullshitters jostling for position to be associated with it.

Where the rubber meets the road
Meaning – from motor racing, the time when something important happens or the point where something starts.
Bullshit – all the preparation in the world counts for nothing until the rubber hits the road…Yuk!

World class
Meaning – outstanding, the best there is.
Bullshit – managers who think they have a world-class team are generally self deluded, lucky or are due for a fall.

BULLSHIT BINGO – Match of the Day

DIFFERENT TEAM IN THE SECOND HALF	BIG MATCH TEMPERAMENT	GOOD PLAYERS DON'T BECOME BAD PLAYERS OVER NIGHT	LETS HIS FOOTBALL DO THE TALKING	WITH THE ADVANTAGE OF TECHNOLOGY	PLAYED OUT OF OUR SKIN	AT THE END OF THE DAY	COULD HAVE GONE EITHER WAY	VALUE OF PUTTING A MAN ON THE POST
FUNNY OLD GAME	THE BOY DONE GOOD	COME OF AGE	TOO GOOD TO GO DOWN	OUR FANS ARE THE BEST IN THE WORLD	ONLY ONE TEAM PLAYED TODAY	HE'S GOT A GOOD ENGINE	SURROUNDED BY CONTROVERSY	THE REAL WINNER TODAY WAS FOOTBALL
BARE BONES	SET OUT THEIR STALL EARLY	DISASTROUS RESULT	DONE FANTASTIC	UNBELIEVABLE	FIRE IN THE BELLY	NATURAL GOAL SCORER	LACK OF SERVICE TO THE FRONT MEN	GREAT FIRST TOUCH
I DIDN'T SEE THE INCIDENT MYSELF	FIGHT TO THE END	ONE GAME AT A TIME	ROLL HIS SLEEVES UP	REFEREE HAD A POOR GAME	EARLY DOORS	GAME OF TWO HALVES	ONLY A COAT OF PAINT BETWEEN HIM AND A GOAL	QUESTION MARKS OVER HIS TEMPERAMENT
CONTROVERSIAL (PENALTY/FREE KICK)	THE BEST TEAM LOST	DRAW A FAIR RESULT	SHUT UP SHOP	GREAT SERVANT TO THE TEAM/GAME	A ROCK IN DEFENCE	HANDBAGS	A GREAT AMBASSADOR FOR THE GAME	LOST A YARD OF PACE...
A SIX POINTER	TWO FOOTED PLAYER	GREAT LEFT/RIGHT PEG	LAST DITCH	DELIVER A QUALITY BALL	PLAYED INTO CONTENTION	SHOCKING	UNFASHIONABLE CLUB	POROUS DEFENCE
FIRST TOUCH LET HIM DOWN	CULTURED RIGHT/LEFT FOOT	CLINICAL FINISH	FULL ON	PLAYS IN THE HOLE	SHODDY	MADE A MEAL OUT OF IT	MIDFIELD GENERAL	DIG IN

How to play: simply tick off seven words in one programme and shout out BINGO!

12. Finance and Accounting

"There are four things that hold back human progress.
Ignorance, stupidity, committees and accountants."

Sir Charles Lyall

Finance and Accounting

The world of finance and accounting is rife with bullshit words and
phrases, but it's a boring world so who can blame them for wanting to
spice it up with a few colourful terms?

Financial people
The finance director runs a company's finance department and apart
from being responsible for **balancing the books**, they're there to
criticise everyone else's work, despite having no experience in any
other job; bizarrely, many FDs end up as the boss. **Bean counter** is a
derogatory name for someone who works in finance and who
apparently has little imagination and though, in many ways, they are
the heroes of this section, keeping bean counters out of business
generally seems a good idea.

Accountants tend to deal with facts and are generally bullshit free, but
don't expect a posh lunch or a day out at the races, cheese sandwiches
and a meeting in the car park is more their idea of a day out. The
most pedantic of finance people are those who would be inclined to
tarmac over their lawn because it's more efficient than gardening; they
should be lumped in with bullshitters and be avoided at all costs.

The numbers

Finance people call their data, spreadsheets, sales or whatever they're working on, 'the numbers'. It's a way of making them seem more important than they really are. Management will say things like 'your numbers look pretty good this week' rather than offer a proper compliment.

When working on their data, the finance people will be **number crunching**, wanting to put over the grind that goes with working something out in detail. Accountants, financially astute managers and finance directors will always present every set of figures, every spread-sheet and every P&L in the light that suits them. The preparation phase is crucial as every factor is looked at; numbers are rounded, stock written off or not included, costs delayed, and the common term for this is **massaging the numbers**. The next stage is **fine tuning**, which applies to the final details around a set of figures that have to be presented; so first the numbers have to be crunched, then massaged and then lastly fine tuned. Mad but true, it's called **creative accounting**. In business, **creative accountancy** is the norm, especially when the company concerned is listed on the stock market and where excuses are needed and figures justified. **Aggressive accountancy** is associated with fraudulent accounting practice but also often applies to companies that follow such rigorous financial policies that they forget about things like keeping customers happy, staff motivation and strategy.

Budgets and forecasting

For finance departments everywhere, their favourite plaything is a **forecast**. They love them, the more the better, updating them endlessly, playing with the various permutations; they particularly enjoy taking the piss out of the poor saps that put the forecast together in the first place. This leads to the **reforecast** which are updates to the original forecast. As the trading year progresses, it's not unusual for retailers to be working to an original budget, a forecast one, a forecast two and also year on year performance. Forecasting is all about guessing how much money will be taken in a given period of time; it's a great opportunity for bullshitters to fix their forecasts in such a way that it shows them in a good light.

Budget setting follows the forecast and they often end up bearing little relationship to each other. The finance department will want to add in other **factors** and **overlay** extra business that they feel the original forecaster has missed. Then they will adapt their **template** (there's always a template) to make the final figure, which will then be adjusted further upwards by the management.

Stretch targets are a favourite addition; there are those **targets** that everyone agrees, then there are those that just go a little further, the theory being that if everyone goes for the stretched target then they'll beat the original ones. It never really works because everyone knows what the real targets are and they'll work to them because it's easier; still, for bullshitters, the only targets that matter are the ones they can crow about hitting. Occasionally a company will come over all experimental and decide to do without a budget, using different targets to stimulate their teams. This will only last about six months before a budget will be introduced and the **bean counters** can sharpen their pencils and go about justifying their jobs once more.

Financially astute bullshitters will use their own language to build a myth around their forecast, saying forecasting isn't **rocket science** or that they're not **robbing Peter to pay Paul** and that **problems are not solved by throwing money at them.**

Classic phrases to watch out for are:

Above (or below) the line
Meaning – above the line on a **profit and loss** account is visible to everyone, below the line is not.
Bullshit – shifting costs below the line is a canny way of boosting profits before tax. Taking costs above the line is a way of proving you

are not a bullshitter and not open to classifying every unforeseen circumstance as **exceptional**.

Back end, Front end

Meaning – back end is to put something off, for example, it may be advantageous to budget sales targets towards the end of the financial year to make early sales look good against budget. A good trick if you know the first part of the year looks tricky, bad if you back end stuff and it doesn't come off. Front end is the opposite when people bring things forward to their advantage.

Bullshit – back end stuff then change jobs before the shit hits the fan, leaving the new guy to take the blame.

Back to basics

Meaning – to return to a fundamental and uncomplicated way of doing something, many companies say this when they've gone through a period of unsuccessful diversification.

Bullshit – usually said when it's too late, by which time people will be saying that other immortal phrase – they should have **stuck to the knitting**…

Bang for the buck

Determining which idea, task, project or deal gives the best return on our time or investments is what most of us do throughout our daily lives. Those who want to look good while going about it ask which options give 'the biggest bang for our buck'… and they're usually leaning back in the wobbly office chair with their hands behind their head, blessed with confidence that they actually look and sound good while saying it.

Better visibility

Meaning – more detail is required, more explanation is needed.

Bullshit – when a manager asks for **better visibility**, they either think that someone's lying to them or in effect they are confessing their ignorance, so while this phrase sounds good, it's not a good bullshit term, unless to expose someone else's bullshit.

Bread and butter
Meaning – a livelihood, the usual way of making money.
Bullshit – there is nothing funny about this term, except the user is probably a boring git.

Building on sand
Meaning – not very stable.
Bullshit – here, a plan or budget is agreed without any basis of fact or substance to the figures, and it may shift considerably from the reality. FDs' and accountants' least favoured emotion is to feel out of control, so say it a few times just to wind them up.

[Not] Comparing apples with apples, Comparing apples and pears
Meaning – comparing two things that aren't alike.
Bullshit – used by the bullshitters who are looking to defend their decisions by comparing figures that aren't really comparable.

Cost effective
Meaning – 'is this worth our while?' A great term used to avoid doing any number of tasks. Asking whether something is cost effective enables the user to delay while investigations take place.
Bullshit – finance people will use this as a challenge, knowing that the challenged will not be able to prove the case either way.

Critical path
Meaning – the critical path is a graphical description of a project or task with each step drawn up and accountabilities marked.
Bullshit – a classic, its great use is for making excuses, apportioning blame and pointing to failure but very occasionally it actually works.

Cut
Meaning – rarely used in public, businesses worldwide have to make cuts occasionally but the act will be dressed up using language such as **downsizing, restructure** and **reorganisation**.
Bullshit – executives seen using this word will be seen as tough and

therefore look good, a great bullshit word then.

Drawing a line in the sand
Meaning – a point at which no more money will be spent.
Bullshit – the line shall not be crossed, no more, no way...

Drivers and levers
The key elements that 'drive' any business, so in retail they are sales, gross profit, stock, margin and, of course, how much money can be screwed out of suppliers. The levers are the actions you take to manage the drivers. It makes sense to them, if no one else.

Exceptional
Meaning – unforeseen, a one off.
Bullshit – normal but unforeseeable costs which the management wish to present as unrepeatable. In fact, something exceptional happens every year.

Gap analysis
Why is there a difference between the real world and the forecast? 'Analyse that gap! No, not that one, the one between your ears...' See *Final score*.

Hand over fist
Meaning – speedily, without control.
Bullshit – a good one for exaggerating problems, 'we're losing money hand over fist'.

In the black/red
In the black is having money, while in the red is overdrawn. While the latter is a common state of affairs to most of the public, it's an excuse for a dressing down in most companies. It's ironic that most people are more careful about their company finances than their own.

Low hanging fruit

Meaning – self preservation may keep you from laughing when this is used, especially without irony, but if your boss says to you that there is no low hanging fruit in your department, take it as a compliment as it means that there were no obvious opportunities to make easy or quick sales or cut costs. The term **Quick win** is a favourite too; it means much the same thing but is less entertaining.

Bullshit – this will be used to give the impression that the facts have been thoroughly investigated and no opportunities are available.

Magic bullet

In desperate times, when their forecasting has failed and they are far from hitting their budget, finance directors are known to prowl their business looking for a solution that will save them and their company, known as the **magic bullet**. The poor fools.

Overview

Meaning – taking in the whole picture, reviewing the entire amount.

Bullshit – it's the finance director's job to take an overview of the total company budget; it's the bullshitter's job to persuade the FD that more funds are diverted to their projects and team.

Playing the percentages

Meaning – the chat up strategy of most single men and also most product manufacturers and suppliers, the hopeful man will ask as many girls out as they can in the hope that one of them will say yes, while the suppliers will produce as many types of products as they can, in the hope that one will sell and enable them to recoup their investment. Watch out for the phrase **chuck enough shit at a wall and some of it will stick**, which has a similar use.

Bullshit – it's standard bullshitter practice whatever the situation.

Pots of gold

Meaning – secret provisions, caches of money.

Bullshit – the company bullshitter keeps these hidden from their boss during budgeting time, in order to bring them in later to hide any errors they may have made or if it looks like they won't hit their targets.

Profit and loss, bottom line
Meaning – the P&L is the account of all costs and sales, but the crucial bit is the **bottom line**, it is accountants' speak for the profit left after all costs and expenditure has been taken into account, in other words, the *bottom line* of the profit and loss account.
Bullshit – generally used by senior managers who want to know the 'bottom line' or, in other words, the answer without the bullshit, therefore a great term to be heard using around the office.

Ring fence
Meaning – put to one side, to be used later.
Bullshit – a typical trick, put some money aside for a specific project, then bring it back when the project fails or isn't signed off. The real aficionados will ring fence money against spurious projects for use in an **arse saving exercise** later.

Rubber stamp
Meaning – give authority, a sign off.
Bullshit – as long as someone else rubber stamps it, then that's fine, unless it's something the company bullshitter wants to take credit for.

The 80/20 rule
Meaning – one of the greatest and most abused rules ever, derived from the work of Italian economist Vilfredo Pareto, his original observation being that 20% of the people had 80% of the wealth. This phrase has been hijacked and the theory applied to many aspects of business. For example, in retail 80% of sales come from 20% of the range, 20% of the stock takes up 80% of the available space, 80% of the work is done by 20% of your staff and so on.
Bullshit – fantastic for excuses and just the use of the word Pareto makes you sound intelligent, even if you've no clue about it.

Top line
Meaning – sales or revenue, the top line of a P&L document.
Bullshit – 'spare me the detail' is a more common meaning these days, which of course leaves more scope for bullshit.

Transparency, Visibility
Meaning – open, nothing hidden, usually to do with company results not hidden by spin or PR bullshit.
Bullshit – and if you believe that you are a complete sucker…

Swings and roundabouts
Meaning – things will even out in the end.
Bullshit – and they usually do…

Tweaking
Meaning – slight adjustments.
Bullshit – financial people always tweak figures right up to the last minute, it's in their nature and they can't help it.

Upside
Meaning – a benefit.
Bullshit – see **pots of gold**.

Wash its face (does it?)
Meaning – does it at least break even?
Bullshit – another stupid expression, in response reply 'yes, and it wipes its own arse as well'. The management is bound to be impressed.

Corporate bullshit
Here's some bullshit that's often applied by financial analysts to a company or by a finance director to describe the situation they're in.

Acquisitions and mergers
Meaning – mostly because one company wants to buy another for the

best price they can, they use terms like these to hide the fact that people are going to lose their jobs and that the company being bought will probably be decimated in the process.

Bullshit – bullshit speak for takeovers.

Asset stripping

Meaning – to ruthlessly sell the assets of a company after an acquisition.

Bullshit – no room for emotion, just make what you can and leave the carcass for others to clear up.

Basket case, Hospital case

Meaning – a term applied to an individual or company that looks like it's going under whatever happens.

Bullshit – the MD of a recovering company will say things like, 'In 1999 we were described as a basket case and now look at us'. This mantra will be repeated often in an effort to convince everyone that it's true, though in reality it often hides inept management. Avoid companies tagged with this unless they have sacked the MD who was in charge at the time. See *Cyclosis*.

Cherry picking

Meaning – choosing the best bits.

Bullshit – picking and choosing those assets to buy in an acquisition and leaving the dross with the vendor. This has achieved a wider meaning in management speak and is used throughout business.

City

The analysts, shareholders and investment people who monitor performance and own shares in public companies. Most MDs of PLCs will spend their waking hours thinking about what the **City** might think of their decisions and subsequent bullshit surrounding the bad ones.

Cyclosis

Meaning – the realisation that the company success over a period of time has been completely due to cyclical factors outside of their control, such as a favourable economic cycle. Imagine presenting this one as a reason for your company's performance to the **City** and shareholders.

Bullshit – a great excuse in certain circumstances, especially for shifting blame.

Dead cat bounce

Meaning – a small and temporary recovery in a market or trading sector following a large fall.

Bullshit – not much worth as a bullshit term, as most people won't know what the hell you're talking about…

Double dip

Meaning – an economist's term applied to a period where, for example, sales have been poor, but for a short while look good, but then go back to performing poorly again, usually for the same reasons as before.

Bullshit – the bullshitter using this will seem as though they know their stuff, always thinking about trends and good with **numbers**.

Double whammy

When two large, usually unfortunate, events happen at once or close together. It originates from a US cartoon called Li'l Abner where the double whammy was an intense stare designed to have a withering effect on whomever it was aimed at.

Downsize

Meaning – to cut, reduce in size.

Bullshit – a way of avoiding saying the word **cut**, now seen as a word used to cover up a multitude of sins. Companies start downsizing when profits go down and overheads go up. The term **down shifting** is also used in this context.

Enronomics
After the Enron Company, this is a company where there is little in the way of proper accounting and fiscal techniques, probably managed by fools and bullshitters in combination.

Equity victim
Someone who, when they lose money on their shares or investments, attempts to blame others for their loss; in reality, it's their own stupid fault for investing in the things in the first place and believing the company bullshit.

Gold plating
Meaning – from the world of company takeovers where the company being bought overplays its value deliberately for a better price.
Bullshit – a recognised behaviour of any bullshitter is to give something lots of benefits so that it appears better than it really is.

Green shoots
Meaning – to show evidence of growth.
Bullshit – this is always mentioned after a company has gone through a tough time, usually after a **bloodbath**, when new management is desperate to find a good news story.

Investor
The sucker that has the money to invest in the bullshit provided by the company, the bullshitters will suck up to the investors using phrases such as great **shareholder value** and **entrepreneurial** investment.

Open the kimono
Meaning – to open the books to auditors, to expose something previously covered up.
Bullshit – amazingly some people actually use this term.

Seedcorn
Meaning – start up funds.
Bullshit – more bullshit is expended in getting money than almost anywhere else, with projections over stated, ambitions too high and people just getting plain greedy.

Slippery slope, downward spiral, tailspin, free fall
Meaning – a fast descent.
Bullshit – usually attributed to companies who are on the way to becoming a basket case, with share prices on a downward spiral, never to recover.

Slush fund
Meaning – a fund of money that isn't allocated to a specific thing or doesn't have a purpose.
Bullshit – often illegal and often very handy in a tight corner.

Negotiations
Companies depend on good negotiators getting the right deal; it's bluff and double bluff and there's no such thing as a win-win situation.

According to research and various training companies, there are four major negotiation styles and types.

1. *Deal maker, trader* – obsessed by the deal, enjoys the process of horse-trading without much concern for the result
2. *Nice, mediator* – likes to form a relationship, enjoys the personal side of negotiating but has a tendency towards naivety
3. *Fighter, hard* – just wants to win no matter who is damaged
4. *Spreadsheet, numerator* – can't deal with people or situations unless they have figures to hand

We've added a fifth:

5. *Bullshitter* – chameleon-like skills, will be able to take on the persona of each of the above as needed, but won't make good negotiators; they lie too much and just complicate things as they don't really care about the deal, only about looking good

Apparently we have an element of each of these traits but some are more dominant than others.

Bridge the gap
Meaning – any negotiator will tell you that a negotiation is about bridging the gap between two parties, it's a standard part of negotiation training.
Bullshit – nowadays more synonymous with the gap between actual sales and the sales budget; commonly the MD (whilst finger jabbing) will be saying '*you* promised me this, now what are *you* going to do to bridge the gap?' Negotiate your way out of that!

Bring to the table, Lay cards on the table
Meaning – what's on offer or what is to be conceded.
Bullshit – nothing much generally.

Bung
Meaning – a bribe, gift or freebie no matter how small.
Bullshit – very useful when doing business in certain parts of the world, such as Swindon.

Do a number on
Meaning – to put one over, take advantage of, exploit.
Bullshit – most negotiators, whether they admit it or not, want to put one over on their opposition.

Done deal
Meaning – finalised agreement.
Bullshit – it's all been agreed and there's no going back. Ha ha.

Legs
Meaning – lasting for a long time.
Bullshit – most negotiators worth their salt negotiate an ending to a deal, usually a year, it keeps them in their jobs.

Nail
Meaning – finalise, complete.
Bullshit – nailing a deal generally means to the advantage of the one doing the nailing…

Partnership
Meaning – working together equally.
Bullshit – if a negotiator starts with the immortal line 'we want this to be a partnership', then you know that they really mean 'we want you to believe it's a partnership but really we want to shaft you'.

Stake in the ground
Meaning – state a specific position.
Bullshit – someone has to start negotiating somewhere and someone has to make the first move in any negotiation…but where to put the stake!

Sunset, Sunrise clause
Meaning – clauses, usually bonuses or termination dates, but at the end or beginning of deals or contracts.
Bullshit – usually they're not worth much but the company bullshitter will always want to sneak a few clauses in just for fun if nothing else.

Ts and Cs
Meaning – terms and conditions.
Bullshit – most companies have a Ts and Cs policy document that they attempt to impose on each other. In English law, the one that applies is the one that was exchanged last, so companies regularly update theirs and send them to each other all the time, especially if there's the likelihood of imminent dispute.

Unwind a deal
Meaning – renegotiate an agreement.
Bullshit – this can involve much grovelling and great negotiation skills as it sometimes indicates that some wally has made a mistake.

Up the ante
Meaning – increase the pressure by increasing a stake, refusing to agree a deal or being tough.
Bullshit – always risky and company bullshitters hate taking risks.

Win-win situation
Meaning – a deal where everyone gets something good out of it, both sides win.
Bullshit – a deal where everyone thinks they're getting something good out of it, both sides think they've won.

BULLSHIT BINGO – Finance

STRETCH TARGET	NUMBER CRUNCHING	BOTTOM LINE	DOWNSIZE	BUILDING ON SAND	STOCK	CUT	FINE TUNING	KPI	MASSAGE THE NUMBERS
BUDGET	BANG FOR THE BUCK	MOVE THE GOAL POSTS	THE CITY	POTS OF GOLD	BENCH-MARKING	MAGIC BULLET	ENTRE-PRENEURIAL	FORECAST	80/20
PLAY THE PERCENTAGES	THE NUMBERS	DOCKING	FAG PACKET	SHAREHOLDER VALUE	CASH FLOW	ROBBING PETER TO PAY PAUL	VISIBILITY	QUICK FIX	TIGHT
IN THE BLACK	IN THE RED	CASH NEUTRAL	GAP ANALYSIS	TOUCH BASE	QUICK AND DIRTY	DOUBLE DIP	INVESTOR	CRITICAL PATH	DOUBLE WHAMMY
TIMING	DEVIL IS IN THE DETAIL	RESULT	LOW HANGING FRUIT	RE-FORECAST	DOWNWARD SPIRAL	RECOVERY	ABOVE THE LINE	SLIPPERY SLOPE	GREEN SHOOTS
COMPARE APPLES WITH APPLES	GAP ANALYSIS	ACTION	CHERRY PICKING	EXCEPTIONAL	BELOW THE LINE	HOSPITAL CASE	SWINGS AND ROUND-ABOUTS	UPLIFT	FREE FALL

How to play: simply tick off six words in one meeting and shout out BINGO!

13. I.T. bullshit

"Technology is dominated by two types of people: those who understand what they do not manage, and those who manage what they do not understand."

Putt's Law

I.T. bullshit
The I.T. department in most companies seems to be a very sad place; people appear to be condemned to installing systems that don't work and when they do work, they have to deal with poor saps that have no clue how to work with them.

It's no wonder that a phone call to the ubiquitous help desk leads to frustration, rudeness and the odd gem of customer service when something is fixed by what seems a stroke of genius to the customer.

Omitting the ever-present jargon, here are a few I.T. derived bullshit classics:

Access
Meaning – right to enter.
Bullshit – I.T. people can get at information that others aren't authorised for; with this in mind, befriending the nerd is a good policy, especially when it comes to revenge.

Bandwidth
Meaning – the amount of data that can be assimilated. A **low bandwidth** meeting is one that hasn't much content or scope; people with

narrow bandwidth are considered too busy to cope – either that or they are just plain stupid.
Bullshit – bullshitters like to control bandwidth.

Connectivity
Meaning – ability to be connected.
Bullshit – hijacked by communicators and marketing people to show how in touch they are with their chosen targets, the company bullshit merchant will be concerned with connectivity to anyone they consider important.

Cut and paste
Meaning – copy and transfer some information to somewhere else, such as another document.
Bullshit – generally all a bit slapdash.

Downtime
Meaning – a period of time when something, either a system of factory, isn't operating i.e. when tools are downed.
Bullshit – this probably isn't a good thing but always a good opportunity to improve scores at Minesweeper.

Eating your own dog food
Meaning – the process of using something that you have created and the realisation that it's rubbish.
Bullshit – if only more managers were subjected to this process, what a nicer world we would live in.

Ego surfing
Meaning – typing your own name into Google to see what comes back.
Bullshit – in theory, bullshitters will ensure that only good things come up when their name is typed in, unless they happen to be called Michael Jackson, but in reality, it's one of the few things they can't control.

Firewall
Meaning – a barrier to prevent fire or attacks on your PC.
Bullshit – managers who talk about firewalls to defend their company or department are generally really referring to themselves.

Fuzzy logic
Meaning – a form of maths used to make decisions when information is imprecise.
Bullshit – a good term to use as a way of disagreeing with someone without calling them stupid or saying they're wrong.

Hand holding
Meaning – to sit with someone while they complete an I.T. task.
Bullshit – ah bless them, but it can also be used to describe any situation where someone is being helped through a task; it might be wise to ask why they're being so helpful…

Integrity
Meaning – stability and soundness of a system.
Bullshit – no matter how good the systems are, personal integrity seems to disappear when the pressure is on and when personal ambitions come into play.

Intranet
Meaning – an internal Internet, with limited access.
Bullshit – in companies that use an intranet, each department generally has its own pages, a great chance to bullshit internally, but few people actually read them.

Jack in
Meaning – to log on.
Bullshit – now used in this context, 'Can you jack in to the youth market and see what they're buying?'

Multi-tasking
Meaning – doing several jobs concurrently.
Bullshit – originally applied to processors, but now used to refer to skills. A person who is good at multi-tasking is generally good at balancing several jobs at once, which means they're usually female. See also **spinning plates** and **ball juggling**.

Ping
Meaning – to send an e-mail.
Bullshit – as a term, just bloody annoying.

Portal
Meaning – a website that acts as a gateway to other websites, a doorway.
Bullshit – another phrase borrowed by business to give the impression that more customers use them than they really do. This book is a portal for bullshit.

State of the art
Meaning – the most up to date technology, best in the industry.
Bullshit – for many companies, state of the art means a colour printer or maybe a shredder, but for others, it's that high-end system that cost a fortune and does nothing it was bought for.

User
Meaning – someone who uses a computer.
Bullshit – mainly a derogatory term for someone who has limited knowledge of how to work a computer, you have to say the word with a sneer to get the full effect.

Viral
Meaning – caused by a virus, in other words, spreads easily.
Bullshit – going viral is a sort of nirvana for many an ad agency as it means success and bonuses all round.

Word of mouse
Meaning – gossip by e-mail.
Bullshit – this usually becomes second or third hand bullshit…

14. Acronyms

"Tracy Barlow! I mean, even her initials are a killer disease!"
Eileen Grimshaw
Coronation Street

Acronyms
Most businesses and industries have their own shorthand and it's a good opportunity for bullshitters to impress with their knowledge. A sad sight, these are the sort of bullshitters who walk around with a load of keys attached to their belts alongside the mobile phone holder in an attempt to make themselves look more important than they really are.

AAA
Meaning – Alive, Alert, Aggressive
Bullshit – this is how the company bullshitter wants to appear.

ACORN
Meaning – A Classification Of Residential Neighbourhoods, invented by CACI Ltd as a way of measuring and classifying consumers.
Bullshit – bandied about by marketing bullshitters in order to give the appearance of expertise.

AFLO
Meaning – Another Fucking Learning Opportunity
Bullshit – one to use when the boss says 'we must learn by our mistakes…'

AFTO
Meaning – Ask For The Order
Bullshit – the equivalent of a knot in a sales person's handkerchief.

AKA
Meaning – Also Known As
Bullshit – the bullshitter, A.K.A. the promising candidate.

AKUTA
Meaning – A Kick Up The Arse
Bullshit – one for the boss.

APE
Meaning – Attentive, Peripheral, Empathic
Bullshit – apparently, this is about listening, sales people must be able to actually listen to their customers' needs rather than just go on about their products.

ASTRO
Meaning – Always Stating The Really Obvious
Bullshit – a typical manager then.

ATNA
Meaning – All Talk No Action
Bullshit – a typical manager then.

B2B
Meaning – Business To Business
Bullshit – used by would be Internet entrepreneurs in order to give the appearance of someone who knows about business.

BOGOFF
Meaning – Buy One Get One For Free
Bullshit – usually a sign that either the retailer or supplier is desperate.

BOHICA
Meaning – Bend Over, Here It Comes Again
Bullshit – a permanent position from most workers, except brown-nosers who tend to adopt another position.

CADET
Meaning – Can't Add, Doesn't Even Try
Bullshit – this applies to most people who work in the finance department who are lost without Excel.

DINKY
Meaning – Double Income No Kids Yet
Bullshit – traditionally the richest group of consumers to be sucked up to.

DNA
Meaning – building block, make up
Bullshit – here the customer's DNA has nothing to do with their biological make up, nor has a company's DNA, or a product for that matter, it all just makes you want to slap whoever uses this term.

DRIB
Meaning – Don't Read If Busy
Bullshit – hard to believe this is actually used but it should be applied to nearly every bit of paper and e-mail ever received.

DTS
Meaning – Danger To Shipping
Bullshit – what is it about some people in offices? They suddenly turn from attractive, young, vibrant individuals to dull, desk bound fatties who in some countries would be classed as a shipping hazard.

EBITDA
Meaning – Earnings Before Interest, Taxes, Depreciation and Amortization

Bullshit – something everyone who owns a company should know but doesn't.

EDLP
Meaning – Every Day Low Pricing, a technique pioneered by supermarkets where they price products in such a way that it looks like they have squeezed every last penny on costs, in order to give the customer a better deal. So items normally priced at £4.99 will be priced at something like £4.83.
Bullshit – you can bet your life that some poor farmer in the third world is paying for the 17p difference and not the supermarket in question.

FIFO
Meaning – First In First Out
Bullshit – applied when culling staff, although other factors are often taken into account such as looks, age, height, hair colour and gullibility.

FMCG
Meaning – Fast Moving Consumer Goods
Bullshit – something executives mention when they want to appear knowledgeable about retail and supermarkets in particular.

FNG
Meaning – Fucking New Guy
Bullshit – a reference to what a pain it is to train up a new person in the office, but then you can give them all the shitty jobs too.

FOBIO
Meaning – Frequently Outwitted By Inanimate Objects
Bullshit – isn't it funny how the most calm, patient people can turn into psychopaths when it comes to adjusting the office chair…

FOC
Meaning – Free Of Charge
Bullshit – in the world of the corporate bullshitter, nothing is FOC.

FOFO
Meaning – Fuck Off and Find Out
Bullshit – well someone is being lazy or stupid or both...

FORCE
Meaning – Focus On Reducing Costs Everywhere
Bullshit – accountants and new finance directors love to make a mark; they do this not by creating revenue but by cutting costs in the hope that everyone will work harder to make up the difference. Invariably in time this ruins the company.

FRO
Meaning – Fuck Right Off
Bullshit – a good old-fashioned negotiation term.

FUBB
Meaning – Fucked Up Beyond Belief
Bullshit – and the company bullshitter is nowhere to be seen.

FUCT
Meaning – Failed Under Continuous Testing
Bullshit – applied especially not to something mechanical but to the poor pleb who has started a job only to find that no one likes them.

FUD
Meaning – Fear, Uncertainty and Doubt
Bullshit – some managers like to breed an atmosphere of FUD as a way to manage people, eventually their team will turn to glorious revenge.

GLAM
Meaning – Greying, Leisured, Affluent, Married
Bullshit – the fastest growing consumer group in the western world and the target of bullshitters everywhere.

IDEAL
Meaning – Identify, Define, Explore, Action, Look back
Bullshit – for problem solving, this is a bit of a classic although no one seems to use it anymore.

IMHO
Meaning – In My Humble Opinion
Bullshit – well it's not humble at all is it? To be lumped in with the classic 'with respect'.

IPATTAP
Meaning – Interrupt, Patronise, Argue, Threaten, Terminate, Apply Penalties
Bullshit – this is presumably what passes for customer service in the banking industry.

JFDI
Meaning – Just Fucking Do It
Bullshit – funnily enough, it's much more satisfying to actually say the words rather than the acronym.

KAS
Meaning – Knowledge, Attitude, Skills
Bullshit – the bullshitter will prefer Cunning, Aptitude, Shite.

KISS
Meaning – Keep It Simple Stupid
Bullshit – one of the most patronising acronyms, so therefore one of the most used.

KPI

Meaning – Key Performance Indicators are the lifeblood of any financial manager; they enable them to monitor how the business is performing to a set of predetermined criteria. Many businesses, when they discover the joys of using KPIs, go mad, overusing them and putting their staff under strain.

Bullshit – the trick is to make sure KPIs are attainable and will never be threatened; if that looks likely, someone else will get the blame.

KVI

Meaning – Known Value Item, a line in a supermarket that everyone knows the value of, for example, bread, milk and baked beans.

Bullshit – most retailers kid themselves about what a KVI is; most suppliers dream of getting a KVI, especially if they are the only ones who supply it.

LANO

Meaning – Lights Are Not On

Bullshit – and no one is home, except the ubiquitous bullshitter.

LAST

Meaning – Listen, Advise, Solve, Thank

Bullshit – a way to deal with problems, bless…

MBO

Meaning – Management By Objectives

Bullshit – objective setters, there's something of the night about them.

MBWA

Meaning – Management By Walking About (or Wandering Around)

Bullshit – a typical management technique or lack of technique depending on your perspective.

MILE

Meaning – Maximum Impact, Little Effort

Bullshit – the bullshitter's motto, or one of them anyway.

MMM
Meaning – Measurable, Manageable, Motivational
Bullshit – Yawn…

NB
Meaning – No Bullshit
Bullshit – No entertainment.

NFG
Meaning – No Fucking Good
Bullshit – one that should be used more often.

PANIC
Meaning – Pressured And Not In Control
Bullshit – a good description for most managers.

PDQ
Meaning – Pretty Damn Quick
Bullshit – not used much these days but effective somehow.

PEBCAK
Meaning – Problem Exists Between Chair And Keyboard
Bullshit – as ever, a bad workman blames his tools.

PICNIC
Meaning – Problem In Chair Not In Computer
Bullshit – these I.T. ones are just so witty…

POS
Meaning – Pile Of Shite
Bullshit – to some this means Point of Sale, we like this version with the alternative being BOS, for Bag O' Shite.

PPPP (The Four Ps)

Meaning – Product, Price, Promotion, Place
Bullshit – one of the retail basics, although estate agents seem to have adopted it as part of their bullshit.

ROI

Meaning – Return On Investment
Bullshit – the corporate bullshitter will always do something for a return, whether it's business or stitching up a colleague.

RTFM

Meaning – Read The Frigging Manual
Bullshit – another one from those helpful guys in the I.T. department.

SISO (Shit In, Shit Out), GIGO (Garbage In, Garbage Out)

Meaning – if you input poor data, you get poor results.
Bullshit – glad to see nothing has changed there then.

SMART

Meaning – Specific, Measurable, Agreed, Realistic, Time-bound
Bullshit – an old favourite used to brainwash young managers everywhere.

SNAFU

Meaning – Situation Normal All Fucked Up
Bullshit – implying that everything is a mess, all the time.

SSDD

Meaning – Same Shit Different Day
Bullshit – depressing or what, anyone saying this deserves all they get…

SWOT

Meaning – Strengths, Weaknesses, Opportunities, Threats
Bullshit – beloved by consultants everywhere.

TEAM

Meaning – Together Everyone Achieves More
Bullshit – when this is said, the speaker usually has their fingers crossed behind their back and are probably thinking 'because then I don't get the blame…'

TFL

Meaning – Too Fucking Late
Bullshit – time for reprisals and **blamestorming**.

TINA

Meaning – There Is No Alternative
Bullshit – for most bullshitters this doesn't apply, they usually have their **exit strategy** all worked out.

TQM

Meaning – Total Quality Management
Bullshit – a blast from the past, management guru jargon from the 1980s, it's included because we miss it.

USP

Meaning – Unique Selling Point (or Proposition)
Bullshit – see *Differentiation*, it's an obsession for some; the bullshitter will be wanting to create a USP of their own to make them stand out.

WOMBAT

Meaning – Waste Of Money, Brains And Time
Bullshit – applies to many.

WYGIWYD

Meaning – What You Get Is What You Deserve
Bullshit – yep, absolutely, although the bullshitter will never think so…

WYSIWYG

Meaning – What You See Is What You Get
Bullshit – people who tell you this applies to them are lying…

BULLSHIT BINGO – Acronyms

JDFI	TEAM	TINA	SSDD	KISS	FMCG	MILE
EDLP	USP	TQM	PDQ	IDEAL	DINKY	PEBCAK
AKA	WSYWIG	WOMBAT	PANIC	FRO	DTS	POS
SISO	AAA	MMM	MBWA	IDEAL	FUD	SMART
SWOT	FIFO	RTFM	LAST	KPI	DNA	RTFM
SNAFU	ROI	GIGO	MBO	FORCE	KAS	PPPP

How to play: simply tick off five acronyms in one meeting and shout out BINGO!

15. The weird and wonderful

"People that are really very weird can get into sensitive positions and have a tremendous impact on history."

Dan Qualye

The weird and wonderful

Here's a selection of the oddest, the most eccentric, the visual and those we just couldn't categorise. It seems that corporate types compete to see who can come out with the strangest and most exotic terms. We have a term of our own for those people, it's not technical, it's fuckwit.

Assmosis
Meaning – from the Dilbert cartoon, a description of the process by which a person climbs the career ladder by sucking up to the boss.
Bullshit – so a good bullshit technique then...

Bo Derek
Meaning – the perfect deal.
Bullshit – this was named after the actress who appeared in the 1979 film *10*, seems a bit out of date now; maybe it should be a Britney or Christina or a Pamela...maybe not.

Checking the pulse, finger on the pulse
Meaning – how things are progressing, the state of play.
Bullshit – all businesses have a heart and can be likened to an organism, so this is a logical term; unfortunately bullshitters have no heart...

Chinese walls
Meaning – a term originated from the 1929 Stock crash where an imagined wall is put up; it is when information trading is prohibited because of mutual interest, say between two companies owned by an umbrella company.
Bullshit – you can almost guarantee it's a complete sham, especially when stakes are high.

Cooking with gas
Meaning – underway, making rapid progress.
Bullshit – 'what the hell is this all about?' Often said by managers who feel something is on the way to being a success. 'Now we're cooking with gas!' Why not electricity or microwaves or nuclear power? Maybe gas just sounds hotter.

Does exactly what it says on the tin
Meaning – from the Ronseal varnish adverts, meaning uncomplicated, easy to interpret and use.
Bullshit – Ronseal products might do this but not much else does...

Dog's bollocks
Meaning – from the premise that a dog is so fond of licking its bollocks, it follows that there must be something pretty bloody good about them. So this phrase means actually something outstanding.
Bullshit – a favourite of senior managers who want to appear as 'one of the lads'; the ones to avoid.

Emperor's new clothes
Meaning – from the Hans Christian Andersen fairy tale, in this context it comes in to play when someone convinces themselves that the value of a valueless object is very high. Also applies when a leader follows a hopeless path with his team backing him even though they all know it will end in failure.
Bullshit – pretty common throughout the corporate world, only in business you don't get a small child pointing out the obvious...

Going postal

Meaning – going mad, especially after something bad happens.
Bullshit – apparently postal workers in America were prone to losing it in a big way because of the stress associated with their jobs; posting letters is stressful is it? Yeah right.

Herding cats

Meaning – impossible.
Bullshit – try it and you'll understand...

Jerry-built

Meaning – shoddy workmanship, made for a quick sale.
Bullshit – sounds like it applies to many listed companies.

Mad as a box of frogs

Meaning – unpredictable, totally barmy.
Bullshit – excellent term that applies to most offices and work situations that involve many departments in a large business.

Pear-shaped

Meaning – gone wrong.
Bullshit – there doesn't seem to be an obvious origin for this term except that maybe something that was meant to be circular went pear shaped; of course, bullshit comes into play when it becomes obvious that plans are going wrong.

Pigs might fly

Meaning – it won't happen, extremely unlikely.
Bullshit – a term that becomes common around bonus time.

Proof of the pudding is in the eating, seeing is believing

Meaning – don't take anything for granted.
Bullshit – good advice all round, bullshit is everywhere.

Put this one to bed
Meaning – finish off, everything dealt with.
Bullshit – the implication being that those involved should move on to something else, many are so eager to go on to the next project it becomes a good opportunity to bury anything unwanted in the last project.

Rule of thumb
Meaning – an often used but an imprecise measurement.
Bullshit – as a general rule of thumb, there's plenty of bullshit to be found in most companies.

Run it up the Flagpole (and see if it gets a salute)
Meaning – to test something to see if it works or gets approved.
Bullshit – a stupid term if ever there was one.

Salmon day
Meaning – one of those days where it feels like you're swimming against the current only to get screwed, then die at the end.
Bullshit – too many of these and it's time to go, change jobs, change your life, change countries…

Smoke and mirrors
Meaning – generally something ephemeral that hides the true situation.
Bullshit – a bullshitter, the spin doctor and the PR people – it's all smoke and mirrors really.

Stick it in the rocket and blast off
Meaning – aggressively start a project once everything is in place.
Bullshit – could you say this in a meeting, with a straight face? Avoid anyone who can.

Talk until blue in the face
Meaning – an attempt to persuade someone of something for a long

time, with no result.
Bullshit – occurs in most meetings.

Ticking time bomb
Meaning – a disaster waiting to happen.
Bullshit – it's amazing how many there are when you look for them; the accomplished bullshitter will be aware of what the major upcoming issues are and will initiate the problem, to either undermine their boss or solve the said problem, becoming a hero in the process.

Tongue in cheek
Meaning – something humorous said in a serious way.
Bullshit – the worst part is when you think it's something said tongue in cheek only to find they meant it, particularly bad if it's your boss.

Up their own arse
Meaning – pretentious, self important.
Bullshit – yep, there are plenty of these people around.

Whistling past the graveyard
Meaning – ignoring a serious or impending problem, while knowing it's really there all the time.
Bullshit – a constant theme through company life, many problems never get addressed until it's too late – bullshit rules.

BULLSHIT BINGO – *The weird and wonderful*

SMOKE AND MIRRORS	WHISTLING PAST THE GRAVEYARD	UP THEIR OWN ARSE	PUT THIS ONE TO BED	STICK IT IN THE ROCKET AND BLAST OFF	DOES EXACTLY WHAT IT SAYS ON THE TIN	RUN IT UP THE FLAGPOLE
GOING POSTAL	TONGUE IN CHEEK	FINGER ON THE PULSE	EMPEROR'S NEW CLOTHES	PROOF OF THE PUDDING…	MAD AS A BOX OF FROGS	COOKING WITH GAS
RULE OF THUMB	CHINESE WALLS	DOG'S BOLLOCKS	HERDING CATS	PIGS MIGHT FLY	TICKING TIME BOMB	BUILDING ON SAND
BANG FOR THE BUCK	DEEP DIVING	ASSMOSIS	SALMON DAY	JERRY-BUILT	DEAD CAT BOUNCE	SQUARING THE CIRCLE
DOG AND PONY SHOW	STRETCH THE ENVELOPE	BLUE SKY THINKING	LOW HANGING FRUIT	RIDING THE RAZOR BLADE	TALK UNTIL BLUE IN THE FACE	EATING YOUR OWN DOG FOOD

How to play: simply tick off five in one meeting and shout out BINGO!

16. Skiving techniques

"Far from idleness being the root of all evil, it is rather the only true good."

Soren Kierkegaard

Skiving techniques
Bullshitting isn't all about ambition, screwing others and getting to the top on their backs, it can also include excuses and crap from those fakes at the other end of the spectrum, the skivers.

Recently it was shown that British workers are outstanding skivers and, by their efforts, can extend non-work time by up to 14 days a year.

1. The cigarette break. This involves finding five minutes several times a day, usually outside or in a designated area to smoke, while non-smoking colleagues carry on working. Non-smokers can pretend to smoke and go for the breaks anyway.

2. Male toilets are often packed with suitable reading material just for the occasion that often warrants a half an hour's break – a good shit.

3. Passing the baton. You are given work to do, you can either ignore it or pass it on to someone else saying that you were asked to hand it to them.

4. Feigning illness, a classic and the most obvious skiving trick, in the last decade it was backache, these days it's stress, which is much less measurable and sometimes if a bullshitter has a hand in it, actually genuine.

5. If approached with some work, always find an excuse to avoid it; ask for a specific form or proof that it's been authorised.

6. Checking out the competition is often a good excuse for a trip abroad or at least to somewhere nicer than the workplace.

7. Create a problem or a crisis; spend all day 'sorting it out'.

8. 'I don't know how that works' or 'I'm not trained in that' are good standbys, as is pretending to be stupid or just keeping quiet.

9. Working from home; this is especially good if you can get your boss to agree to you taking a regular working at home day. 'It's amazing how much I get done when there are no distractions…'

10. Being aware of who generates the work, plan your route to your desk so that you avoid them. Try to situate yourself in such a way that you can't be seen. Do just enough work to pass the minimum standard required.

11. Ensure that your PC screen is not seen by anyone; this will enable you to spend days surfing (make sure you go through Google rather than type directly into the web browser, it's less likely to be picked up), playing games, gambling, trading on e-Bay and e-mailing friends.

12. Working lunches and coffee breaks are always extendable and difficult to check up on; just don't go back to the office if you're too pissed.

13. Work is often so boring it induces sleepiness and you may find the need for a doze, the loo can be busy and uncomfortable, so find some place cosy such as under your desk but take an object with you such as a pen, then if you're woken up by someone, you can be just looking for the pen you'd 'dropped' earlier.

Acknowledgements

Here are just a few words of gratitude...

I'd particularly like to thank Paul Torjussen of Southbank for his backing, encouragement and large cheque...when it arrives.

My thanks also to all those people and colleagues who suggested many of the terms that appear in this book, everyone seems to have a favourite.

Thanks in particular to the now expelled management at my previous company, who were so full of it.

Big thanks to Carl Newbrook, a true gent and fellow bullshit collector.

A very big 'thank you' also goes to Charles Powiesnik without whom this book would not have been written.

Lastly to Michaela for all else that matters.

BULLSHIT NOTES

List your own company bullshit classics on these pages. A blank card is provided at the back of the book to create your own game.

Why not send us a copy of your bullshit classics to bullshit@southbankpublishing.com

BULLSHIT NOTES

CONFESSIONS OF AN ADVERTISING MAN

'Ultimately, this book is important because it's not just about advertising, it's also about how people think and behave at the sharp end of business-any business'.

Sir Alan Parker

'Required reading for anyone in the business'

Media Week

'Ogilvy the creative force of modern advertising'

The New York Times

The international best seller is available again from Southbank Publishing. David Ogilvy was an advertising genius and his views are timeless. If you aspire to be a good manager in any kind of business then this is a must read.

To order your copy
£9.99 including free postage and packing (UK and Eire only),
£12.99 for overseas orders.

For credit card orders phone Turnaround Customers Services on 020 8829 3000 quoting reference 1904915

For orders via post – Cheques payable to Southbank Publishing, 21 Great Ormond St, London, WC1 N 3JB, mail to: Info@southankpublising.com